D1220301

# CLIO, A MUSE
## AND OTHER ESSAYS

# CLIO, A MUSE

## *AND OTHER ESSAYS*

*by*

## GEORGE MACAULAY TREVELYAN

REGIUS PROFESSOR OF MODERN HISTORY IN THE
UNIVERSITY OF CAMBRIDGE

NEW EDITION

*Essay Index Reprint Series*

 **BOOKS FOR LIBRARIES PRESS**
FREEPORT, NEW YORK

NEW EDITION First Published 1930
Reprinted 1968

LIBRARY OF CONGRESS CATALOG CARD NUMBER:
68-20345

PRINTED IN THE UNITED STATES OF AMERICA

TO
WALTER MORLEY FLETCHER

# PREFACE

Most of these pieces have appeared in book form: first in Messrs Longmans' *Clio, a Muse*, 1913, and then in Messrs Nelson's *Recreations of an Historian*, 1919, when *Englishmen and Italians* and *The News of Ramillies* were added to the other essays. The essays have now returned into the hands of Messrs Longmans, who issue them with a few omissions and with the addition of three pieces—*John Bunyan*, *History and Fiction*, and my Inaugural Lecture given at Cambridge in 1927, entitled *The Present Position of History*. This last I have printed at the end of the volume, immediately after an old essay on the same subject, entitled *Clio, a Muse*. When that essay came out in a magazine a quarter of a century ago it was a youthful rebel. For all its crudity I think I will send it out again to parade the streets a little longer with its flag of revolt, but in company with a kind and elderly policeman, my Inaugural Lecture of 1927.

Cambridge,
*July 1929.*

# CONTENTS

WIND of the morning, wind of the gloaming, wind of the night,
What is it that you whisper to the moor
All the day long and every day and year,
Resting and whispering, rustling and whispering, hastening and
  whispering
Around, across, beneath
The tufts and hollows of the listening heath?

GEOFFREY YOUNG, *Wind and Hill.*

# WALKING

" La chose que je regrette le plus, dans les détails de ma vie dont j'ai perdu la mémoire, est de n'avoir pas fait des journaux de mes voyages. Jamais je n'ai tant pensé, tant existé, tant vécu, tant été moi, si j'ose ainsi dire, que dans ceux que j'ai faits seul et à pied."—ROUSSEAU, *Confessions*, I. iv.

" When you have made an early start, followed the coastguard track on the slopes above the cliffs, struggled through the gold and purple carpeting of gorse and heather on the moors, dipped down into quaint little coves with a primitive fishing village, followed the blinding whiteness of the sands round a lonely bay, and at last emerged upon a headland where you can settle into a nook of the rocks, look down upon the glorious blue of the Atlantic waves breaking into foam on the granite, and see the distant sea-levels glimmering away till they blend imperceptibly into cloudland; then you can consume your modest sandwiches, light your pipe, and feel more virtuous and thoroughly at peace with the universe than it is easy even to conceive yourself elsewhere. I have fancied myself on such occasions a felicitous blend of poet and saint—which is an agreeable sensation. What I wish to point out, however, is that the sensation is confined to the walker."—LESLIE STEPHEN, *In Praise of Walking*.

I HAVE two doctors, my left leg and my right. When body and mind are out of gear (and those twin parts of me live at such close quarters that the one always catches melancholy from the other) I know that I have only to call in my doctors and I shall be well again.

Mr Arnold Bennett has written a religious tract called *The Human Machine*. Philosophers and clergymen are always discussing why we should be good—as if anyone doubted that he ought to be. But Mr Bennett has tackled the real problem of ethics and religion—how we can make ourselves be good. We all of us know that we ought to be cheerful to ourselves and kind to others, but cheerfulness is often and kindness sometimes as unattainable as sleep in a white night. That combination of mind and body which I call my soul is often so choked up with bad thoughts or useless worries that

> " Books and my food, and summer rain,
> Knock on my sullen heart in vain."

# WALKING

It is then that I call in my two doctors to carry me off for the day.

Mr Bennett's recipe for the blue devils is different. He proposes a course of mental " Swedish exercises," to develop by force of will the habit of " concentrating thought " away from useless angers and obsessions and directing it into clearer channels. This is good, and I hope that everyone will read and practise Mr Bennett's precepts. It is good, but it is not all. For there are times when my thoughts, having been duly concentrated on the right spot, refuse to fire, and will think nothing except general misery; and such times, I suppose, are known to all of us.

On these occasions my recipe is to go for a long walk. My thoughts start out with me like bloodstained mutineers debauching themselves on board the ship they have captured, but I bring them home at nightfall, larking and tumbling over each other like happy little Boy Scouts at play, yet obedient to every order to " concentrate " for any purpose Mr Bennett or I may wish.

> " A Sunday well spent
> Means a week of content."

That is, of course, a Sunday spent with both legs swinging all day over ground where grass or heather grows. I have often known the righteous forsaken and his seed begging for bread, but I never knew a man go for an honest day's walk, for whatever distance, great or small, his pair of compasses could measure out in the time, and not have his reward in the repossession of his own soul.

In this medicinal use of Walking, as the Sabbath-day refection of the tired town worker, companionship is good, and the more friends who join us on the tramp the merrier. For there is not time, as there is on the longer holiday or walking tour, for body and mind to attain that point of training when the higher ecstasies of Walking are felt through the whole being, those joys that crave silence and solitude. And, indeed, on these humbler occasions

# WALKING

the first half of the day's walk, before the Human Machine has recovered its tone, may be dreary enough without the laughter of good company, ringing round the interchange of genial and irresponsible verdicts on the topics of the day. For this reason informal Walking societies should be formed among friends in towns, for week-end or Sabbath walks in the neighbouring country. I never get better talk than in these moving Parliaments, and good talk is itself something.

But here I am reminded of a shrewd criticism directed against such talking patrols by a good walker who has written a book on Walking.[1] " In such a case," writes Mr Sidgwick—" in such a case walking goes by the board; the company either loiters and trails in clenched controversy, or, what is worse sacrilege, strides blindly across country like a herd of animals, recking little of whence they come or whither they are going, desecrating the face of nature with sophism and inference and authority, and regurgitated Blue Book. At the end of such a day what have they profited? Their gross and perishable physical frames may have been refreshed : their less gross but equally perishable minds may have been exercised: but what of their immortal being? It has been starved between the blind swing of the legs below and the fruitless flickering of the mind above, instead of receiving, through the agency of quiet mind and a co-ordinated body, the gentle nutriment which is its due."

Now this passage shows that the author thoroughly understands the high, ultimate end of Walking, which is indeed something other than to promote talk. But he does not make due allowance for times, seasons and circumstances. You cannot do much with your " immortal soul " in a day's walk in Surrey between one fortnight's work in London and the next; if " body " can be " refreshed " and " mind exercised," it is as much as can be hoped for. The perfection of Walking, such as Mr Sidgwick describes in the last sentence quoted, requires longer time, more perfect

[1] Sidgwick, *Walking Essays*, pp. 10-11.

# WALKING

training, and, for some of us at least, a different kind of scenery. Meanwhile let us have good talk as we tramp the lanes.

Nursery lore tells us that " Charles I. walked and talked : half-an-hour after his head was cut off." Mr Sidgwick evidently thinks that it was a case not merely of *post hoc* but *propter hoc*, an example of summary but just punishment. Yet, if I read Cromwell aright, he no less than his royal victim would have talked as he walked. And Cromwell reminds me of Carlyle, who carried the art of " walking and talking " to perfection as one of the highest of human functions. Who does not remember his description of " the sunny summer afternoon " when he and Irving " walked and talked a good sixteen miles "? Those who have gone walks with Carlyle tell us that then most of all the fire kindled. And because he talked well when he walked with others, he felt and thought all the more when he walked alone, " given up to his bits of reflections in the silence of the moors and hills." He was alone when he walked his fifty-four miles in the day, from Muirkirk to Dumfries, " the longest walk I ever made," he tells us. Carlyle is in every sense a patron saint of Walking, and his vote is emphatically given *not* for the " gospel of silence "!

Though I demand silent walking less, I desire solitary walking more than Mr Sidgwick. Silence is not enough; I must have solitude for the perfect walk, which is very different from the Sunday tramp. When you are really *walking*,[1] the presence of a companion, involving such irksome considerations as whether the pace suits him, whether he wishes to go up by the rocks or down by the burn, still more the haunting fear that he may begin to talk, disturbs the harmony of body, mind and soul when they stride along no longer conscious of their separate, jarring entities, made one together in mystic union with the earth, with the hills that still beckon, with the sunset that still shows the tufted

---

[1] Is there the same sort of difference between *tramping* and *walking* as between *paddling* and *rowing*, *scrambling* and *climbing*?

4

moor under foot, with old darkness and its stars that take you to their breast with rapture when the hard ringing of heels proclaims that you have struck the final road.

Yet even in such high hours a companion may be good, if you like him well, if you know that he likes you and the pace, and that he shares your ecstasy of body and mind. Even as I write, memories are whispering at my ear how disloyal I am thus to proclaim only solitary walks as perfect. There comes back to me an evening at the end of a stubborn day, when, full of miles and wine, we two were striding towards San Marino over the crest of a high limestone moor—trodden of old by better men in more desperate mood—one of us stripped to the waist, the warm rain falling on our heads and shoulders, our minds become mere instruments to register the goodness and harmony of things, our bodies an animated part of the earth we trod.

And again, from out of the depth of days and nights gone by and forgotten, I have a vision, not forgettable, of making the steep ascent to Volterra, for the first time, under the circlings of the stars; the smell of unseen almond blossom in the air; the lights of Italy far below us; ancient Tuscany just above us, where we were to sup and sleep, guarded by the giant walls. Few went to Volterra then; but years have passed, and now I am glad to think that many go, *faute de mieux*, in motor-cars; yet so they cannot hear the silence we heard, or smell the almond blossom we smelt, and if they did they could not feel them as the walker can feel. On that night was companionship dear to my heart, as also on the evening when together we lifted the view of distant Trasimene, being full of the wine of Papal Pienza and striding on to a supper washed down by Monte Pulciano, itself drawn straight from its native cellars.

Be not shocked, temperate reader! In Italy wine is not a luxury of doubtful omen, but a necessary part of that good country's food. And if you have walked twenty-five miles and are going on again afterwards, you can imbibe Falstaffian potions and still be as lithe and ready for the field as Prince Hal at Shrewsbury. Remember also that in the Latin village tea is in default. And how could you walk the last ten miles without tea? By a providential ordering wine in Italy is like tea in England, recuperative and innocent of later reaction. Then, too, there are wines in remote Tuscan villages that a cardinal might envy, wines which travel not, but century after century pour forth their nectar for a little clan of peasants, and for any wise English youth who knows that Italy is to be found scarcely in her picture galleries and not at all in her cosmopolite hotels.

Central Italy is a paradise for the walker. I mean the district between Rome and Bologna, Pisa and Ancona, with Perugia for its headquarters, the place where so many of the walking tours of Umbria, Tuscany and the Marches can be ended or begun.[1] The " olive-sandalled Apennine " is a land always of great views, and at frequent intervals of enchanting detail. It is a land of hills and mountains, unenclosed, open in all directions to the wanderer at will, unlike some British mountain game-preserves. And, even in the plains, the peasant, unlike some south-English farmers, never orders you off his ground, not even out of his olive grove or vineyard. Only the vineyards in the suburbs of large towns are concealed, reasonably enough, between high white walls. The peasants are kind and generous to the wayfarer. I walked alone in those parts with great success before I knew more than twenty words of Italian. The pleasure of losing your way on those hills leads to a push over broken ground to a glimmer of light that proves to come from some lonely farmstead, with the family gathered round the burning brands, in honest, cheerful poverty. They will, without bargain or demur, gladly show you the way across the brushwood moor, till the lights of Gubbio are seen beckoning down in the valley beneath. And Italian towns when you enter them, though it be at midnight, are

---

[1] The ordnance maps of Italy can be obtained by previous order at London geographers, time allowed, or else bought in Milan or Rome—and sometimes it is possible to get the local ordnance maps in smaller towns.

still half awake, and everyone volunteers in the search to find you bed and board.

April and May are the best walking months for Italy. Carry water in a flask, for it is sometimes ten miles from one well to the next that you may chance to find. A siesta in the shade for three or four hours in the midday heat, to the tune of cicada and nightingale, is not the least pleasant part of all; and that means early starting and night walking at the end, both very good things. The stars out there rule the sky more than in England, big and lustrous with the honour of having shone upon the ancients and been named by them. On Italian mountain-tops we stand on naked, pagan earth, under the heaven of Lucretius:

" Luna, dies, et nox, et noctis signa severa."

The chorus-ending from Aristophanes' *Frogs*, raised every night from every ditch that drains into the Mediterranean, hoarse and primæval as the raven's croak, is one of the grandest tunes to walk by. Or on a night in May one can walk through the too rare Italian forests for an hour on end and never be out of hearing of the nightingale's song.

Once in every man's youth there comes the hour when he must learn, what no one ever yet believed save on the authority of his own experience, that the world was not created to make him happy. In such cases, as in that of Teufelsdröckh, grim Walking's the rule. Every man must once at least in life have the great vision of Earth as Hell. Then, while his soul within him is molten lava that will take some lifelong shape of good or bad when it cools, let him set out and walk, whatever the weather, wherever he is, be it in the depths of London, and let him walk grimly, well if it is by night, to avoid the vulgar sights and faces of men, appearing to him, in his then dæmonic mood, as base beyond all endurance. Let him walk until his flesh curse his spirit for driving it on, and his spirit spend its rage on his flesh in forcing it still pitilessly to sway the legs. Then the fire within him will not turn to soot and choke him, as it chokes those who linger at home with their grief, motionless, between four mean, lifeless walls. The stricken one who has, more wisely, taken to road and field, as he plies his solitary pilgrimage day after day, finds that he has with him a companion with whom he is not ashamed to share his grief, even the Earth he treads, his mother who bore him. At the close of a well-trodden day grief can have strange visions and find mysterious comforts. Hastening at droop of dusk through some remote by-way never to be found again, a man has known a row of ancient trees nodding over a high stone wall above a bank of wet earth, bending down their sighing branches to him as he hastened past for ever, to whisper that the place knew it all centuries ago and had always been waiting for him to come by, even thus, for one minute in the night.

Be grief or joy the companion, in youth and in middle age, it is only at the end of a long and solitary day's walk that I have had strange, casual moments of mere sight and feeling more vivid and less forgotten than the human events of life, moments like those that Wordsworth has described as his common companions in boyhood, like that night when he was rowing on Esthwaite, and that day when he was nutting in the woods. These come to me only after five-and-twenty miles. To Wordsworth they came more easily, together with the power of expressing them in words! Yet even his vision and power were closely connected with his long daily walks. De Quincey tells us: " I calculate, upon good data, that with these identical legs Wordsworth must have traversed a distance of 175,000 or 180,000 English miles, a mode of exertion which to him stood in the stead of alcohol and all stimulants whatsoever to the animal spirits; to which indeed he was indebted for a life of unclouded happiness, and we for much of what is most excellent in his writings."

There are many schools of Walking and none of them orthodox. One school is that of the road-walkers, the

# WALKING

Puritans of the religion. A strain of fine ascetic rigour is in these men, yet they number among them at least two poets.[1] Stevenson is *par excellence* their bard :

" Boldly he sings, to the merry tune he marches."

It is strange that Edward Bowen, who wrote the Harrow songs, left no walking songs, though he himself was the king of the roads. Bowen kept at home what he used to call his " road-map," an index outline of the ordnance survey of our island, ten miles to the inch, on which he marked his walks in red ink. It was the chief pride of his life to cover every part of the map with those red spider-webs. With this end in view he sought new ground every holiday, and walked not merely in chosen hill and coast districts, but over Britain's dullest plains. He generally kept to the roads, partly in order to cover more ground, partly, I suppose, from preference for the free and steady sway of leg over level surface which attracts Stevenson and all devotees of the road. He told me that twenty-five miles was the least possible distance even for a slack day. He was certainly one of the Ironsides.

To my thinking, the road-walkers have grasped one part of the truth. The road is invaluable for pace and swing,

[1] Of the innumerable poets who were walkers we know too little to judge how many of them were *road*-walkers. Shakespeare, one gathers, preferred the footpath way with stiles to either the highroad or the moor. Wordsworth preferred the lower fell tracks, above the highroads and below the tops of the hills. Shelley we can only conceive of as bursting over or through all obstacles cross-country ; we know he used to roam at large over Shotover and in the Pisan forest. Coleridge is known to have walked alone over Scafell, but he also seems to have experienced after his own fashion the sensations of night-walking on roads :

" Like one that on a lonesome road
Doth walk in fear and dread,
And having once turned round walks on
And turns no more his head ;
Because he knows a frightful fiend
Doth close behind him tread."

There is a " personal note " in that ! Keats, Matthew Arnold and Meredith, there is evidence, were " mixed " walkers—on and off the road.

# WALKING

and the ideal walk permits or even requires a smooth surface for some considerable portion of the way. On other terms it is hard to cover a respectable distance, and the change of tactile values underfoot is agreeable.

But more than that I will not concede: twenty-five or thirty miles of moor and mountain, of wood and field-path, is better in every way than five-and-thirty, or even forty, hammered out on the road. Early in life, no doubt, a man will test himself at pace Walking, and then of course the road must be kept. Every aspiring Cantab and Oxonian ought to walk to the Marble Arch at a pace that will do credit to the college whence he starts at break of day [1]: the wisdom of our ancestors, surely not by an accident, fixed those two seats of learning each at the same distance from London, and at exactly the right distance for a test walk. And there is a harder test than that: if a man can walk the eighty miles from St Mary Oxon to St Mary Cantab in the twenty-four hours, he wins his place with Bowen and a very few more.

But it is a great mistake to apply the rules of such test Walking on roads to the case of ordinary Walking. The secret beauties of nature are unveiled only to the cross-country walker. Pan would not have appeared to Pheidippides on a road. On the road we never meet the " moving accidents by flood and field ": the sudden glory of a woodland glade; the open back-door of the old farmhouse sequestered deep in rural solitude; the cow routed up from meditation behind the stone wall as we scale it suddenly; the deep, slow, south-country stream that we must jump, or wander along to find the bridge; the northern torrent of molten peat-hag that we must ford up to the waist, to scramble, glowing warm-cold, up the farther foxglove bank; the autumnal dew on the bracken and the blue straight smoke of the cottage in the still glen at dawn; the rush down the mountain-side, hair flying, stones and grouse

[1] Start at five from Cambridge, and have a second breakfast ordered beforehand at Royston to be ready at eight.

10

rising at our feet; and at the bottom the plunge in the pool below the waterfall, in a place so fair that kings should come from far to bathe therein—yet is it left, year in year out, unvisited save by us and " troops of stars." These, and a thousand other blessed chances of the day, are the heart of Walking, and these are not of the road.

Yet the hard road plays a part in every good walk, generally at the beginning and at the end. Nor must we forget the " soft " road, mediating as it were between his hard artificial brother and wild surrounding nature. The broad grass lanes of the low country, relics of mediæval wayfaring; the green, unfenced moorland road; the derelict road already half gone back to pasture; the common farm track —these and all their kind are a blessing to the walker, to be diligently sought out by help of map [1] and used as long as may be. For they unite the speed and smooth surface of the harder road with much at least of the softness to the foot, the romance and the beauty of cross-country routes.

It is well to seek as much variety as is possible in twelve hours. Road and track, field and wood, mountain, hill, and plain should follow each other in shifting vision. The finest poem on the effect of variation in the day's walk is George Meredith's *The Orchard and the Heath*. Some kinds of country are in themselves a combination of different delights, as for example the sub-Lake district, which walkers often see in Pisgah view from Bowfell or the Old Man, but too seldom traverse. It is a land sounding with streams from the higher mountains, itself composed of little hills and tiny plains covered half by hazel woods and heather moors, half by pasture and cornfields; and in the middle of the fields rise lesser islands of rocks and patches of the northern jungle still uncleared. The districts along the foot of mountain ranges are often the most varied in feature, and therefore the best for Walking.

[1] Compass and coloured half-inch Bartholomew is the walker's *vade mecum* in the north; the one-inch ordnance is more desirable for the more enclosed and less hilly south of England.

# WALKING

Variety, too, can be obtained by losing the way—a half-conscious process, which in a sense can no more be done of deliberate purpose than falling in love. And yet a man can sometimes very wisely let himself drift, either into love or into the wrong path out walking. There is a joyous mystery in roaming on, reckless where you are, into what valley, road or farm chance and the hour is guiding you. If the place is lonely and beautiful, and if you have lost all count of it upon the map, it may seem a fairy glen, a lost piece of old England that no surveyor would find though he searched for it a year. I scarcely know whether most to value this quality of aloofness and magic in country I have never seen before, and may never see again, or the familiar joys of Walking grounds where every tree and rock are rooted in the memories that make up my life.

Places where the fairies might still dwell lie for the most part west of Avon. Except the industrial plain of Lancashire the whole west, from Cornwall to Carlisle, is, when compared to the east of our island, more hilly, more variegated, and more thickly strewn with old houses and scenes unchanged since Tudor times. The Welsh border, on both sides of it, is good ground. If you would walk away for a while out of modern England, back and away for twice two hundred years, arrange so that a long day's tramp may drop you at nightfall off the Black Mountain on to the inn that nestles in the ruined tower of old Llanthony. Then go on through

> " Clunton and Clunbury, Clungunford and Clun,
>   The quietest places under the sun,"

still sleeping their Saxon sleep, with one drowsy eye open for the " wild Welsh " on the " barren mountains " above. Follow more or less the line of Offa's Dyke, which passes, a disregarded bank, through the remotest loveliness of gorse-covered down and thick, trailing vegetation of the valley bottoms. Or, if you are more leisurely, stay a week at Wigmore till you know the country round by heart.

# WALKING

You will carry away much, among other things considerable scepticism as to the famous sentence at the beginning of the third chapter of Macaulay's *History*: "Could the England of 1685 be, by some magical process, set before our eyes, we should not know one landscape in a hundred, or one building in ten thousand." It is doubtful even now, and I suspect that it was a manifest exaggeration when it was written two generations ago. But Macaulay was not much of a walker across country.[1]

One time with another I have walked twice at least round the coast of Devon and Cornwall, following for the most part the track along the cliff. The joys of this method of proceeding have been celebrated by Leslie Stephen in the paragraph quoted at the head of this essay. But I note that he used to walk there in the summer, when the heather was "purple." I prefer Easter for that region, because when spring comes to deliver our island, like the Prince of Orange he lands first in the south-west. That is when the gorse first smells warm on the cliff-top. Then, too, is the season of daffodils and primroses, which are as native to the creeks of Devon and Cornwall as the scalded cream itself. When the heather is "purple" I will look for it elsewhere.

If the walker seeks variety of bodily motion, other than the run down hill, let him scramble. Scrambling is an integral part of Walking, when the high ground is kept all day in a mountain region. To know and love the texture of rocks we should cling to them; and when mountain-ash or holly, or even the gnarled heather root, has helped us at a pinch, we are thenceforth on terms of affection with all their kind. No one knows how sun and water can make a steep bank of moss smell all ambrosia till he has dug foot, fingers and face into it in earnest. And you must learn to haul yourself up a rock before you can visit those fern-clad inmost secret places where the Spirit of the Gully dwells.

It may be argued that scrambling and its elder brother

[1] Like Shelley, he used to *read* as he walked. I do not think Mr Sidgwick would permit that!

climbing are the essence of Walking made perfect. I am not a climber and cannot judge. But I acknowledge in the climber the one person who, upon the whole, has not good reason to envy the walker. On the other hand, those stalwart Britons who, for their country's good, shut themselves up in one flat field all day and play there, surrounded by ropes and a crowd, may keep themselves well and happy, but they are divorced from nature. Shooting does well when it draws out into the heart of nature those who could not otherwise be induced to go there. But shooters may be asked to remember that the moors give as much health and pleasure to others who do not carry guns. They may, by the effort of a very little imagination, perceive that it is not well to instruct their gamekeepers to turn every one off the most beautiful grounds in Britain on those three hundred and fifty days in the year when they themselves are not shooting. Their actual sport should not be disturbed, but there is no sufficient reason for this dog-in-the-manger policy when they are not using the moors. The closing of moors is a bad habit that is spreading in some places, though I hope it is disappearing in others. It is extraordinary that a man not otherwise selfish should prohibit the pleasures of those who delight in the moors for their own sakes, on the offchance that he and his guests may kill another stag, or a dozen more grouse in the year. And in most cases an occasional party on the moor makes no difference to the grouse at all. The Highlands have very largely ceased to belong to Britain on account of the deer, and we are in danger of losing the grouse moors as well. If the Alps were British they would long ago have been closed on account of the chamois.

The energetic walker can of course in many cases despise notice-boards and avoid gamekeepers on the moors, but I put in this plea on behalf of the majority of holiday-makers, including women and children. One would have thought that mountains as well as seas were a common pleasure ground. But let us register our thanks to the many who do not close their moors.

# WALKING

And the walker, on his side, has his social duties. He must be careful not to leave gates open, not to break fences, not to walk through hay or crops, and not to be rude to farmers. In the interview always try to turn away wrath, and in most cases you will succeed.

A second duty is to burn or bury the fragments that remain from lunch. To find the neighbourhood of a stream-head, on some well-known walking route like Scafell, littered with soaked paper and the relics of the feast is disgusting to the next party. And this brief act of reverence should never be neglected, even in the most retired nooks of the world. For all nature is sacred, and in England there is none too much of it.

Thirdly, though we should trespass we should trespass only so as to temper law with equity. Private gardens and the immediate neighbourhood of inhabited houses must be avoided or only crossed when there is no fear of being seen. All rules may be thus summed up: " Give no man, woman or child just reason to complain of your passage."

If I have praised wine in Italy, by how much more shall I praise tea in England!—the charmed cup that prolongs the pleasure of the walk and its actual distance by the last, best spell of miles. Before modern times there was Walking, but not the perfection of Walking, because there was no tea. They of old time said, " The traveller hasteth towards evening," but it was then from fear of robbers and the dark, not from the joy of glad living, as with us who swing down the darkling road refreshed by tea. When they reached the forest of Arden, Rosalind's spirits and Touchstone's legs were weary—but if only Corin could have produced a pot of tea they would have walked on singing till they found the Duke at dinner. In that scene Shakespeare put his unerring finger fine on the want of his age—tea for walkers at evening.

Tea is not a native product, but it has become our native drink, procured by our English energy at seafaring and trading, to cheer us with the sober courage that fits us best. No, let the swart Italian crush his grape! But grant to me, ye Muses, for heart's ease, at four o'clock or five, wasp-waisted with hunger and faint with long four miles an hour, to enter the open door of a lane-side inn and ask the jolly hostess if she can give me three boiled eggs with my tea— and let her answer " yes." Then for an hour's perfect rest and recovery, while I draw from my pocket some small, well-thumbed volume, discoloured by many rains and rivers, so that some familiar, immortal spirit may sit beside me at the board. There is true luxury of mind and body! Then on again into the night if it be winter, or into the dusk falling or still but threatened—joyful, a man remade.

Then is the best yet to come, when the walk is carried on into the night, or into the long, silent, twilight hours which in the northern summer stand in night's place. Whether I am alone or with one fit companion, then most is the quiet soul awake; for then the body, drugged with sheer health, is felt only as a part of the physical nature that surrounds it and to which it is indeed akin; while the mind's sole function is to be conscious of calm delight. Such hours are described in Meredith's *Night Walk*:

> " A pride of legs in motion kept
> Our spirits to their task meanwhile,
> And what was deepest dreaming slept:
> The posts that named the swallowed mile;
> Beside the straight canal the hut
> Abandoned; near the river's source
> Its infant chirp; the shortest cut;
> The roadway missed were our discourse;
> At times dear poets, when some view
> Transcendent or subdued evoked . . .
> *But most the silences were sweet!* "

Indeed the only reason, other than weakness of the flesh, for not always walking until late at night, is the joy of making a leisurely occupation of the hamlet that chance or whim has selected for the night's rest. There is much merit in the stroll after supper, hanging contemplative at sunset over the little bridge, feeling at one equally with the geese there on the common and with the high gods at rest on Olympus. After a day's walk everything has twice its usual value. Food and drink become subjects for epic celebration, worthy of the treatment Homer gave them. Greed is sanctified by hunger and health. And as with food, so with books. Never start on a walking tour without an author whom you love. It is criminal folly to waste your too rare hours of perfect receptiveness on the magazines that you may find cumbering the inn. No one, indeed, wants to read much after a long walk; but for a few minutes, at supper or after it, you may be in the seventh heaven with a scene of *Henry IV.*, a chapter of Carlyle, a dozen " Nay, Sirs " of Dr Johnson, or your own chosen novelist. Their wit and poetry acquire all the richness of your then condition, and that evening they surpass even their own gracious selves. Then, putting the volume in your pocket, go out, and godlike watch the geese.

On the same principle it is good to take a whole day off in the middle of a walking tour. It is easy to get stale, yet it is a pity to shorten a good walk for fear of being tired next day. One day off in a well-chosen hamlet, in the middle of a week's " hard," is often both necessary to the pleasure of the next three days, and good in itself in the same kind of excellence as that of the evening just described. All day long, as we lie *perdu* in wood or field, we have perfect laziness and perfect health. The body is asleep like a healthy infant—or, if it must be doing for one hour of the blessed day, let it scramble a little; while the powers of mind and soul are at their topmost strength and yet are not put forth, save intermittently and casually, like a careless giant's hand. Our modern life requires such days of " anti-worry," and they are only to be obtained in perfection when the body has been walked to a standstill.

George Meredith once said to me that we should " love all changes of weather." That is a true word for walkers.

# WALKING

Change in weather should be made as welcome as change in scenery. "Thrice blessed is our sunshine after rain." I love the stillness of dawn, and of noon, and of evening, but I love no less the "winds austere and pure." The fight against fiercer wind and snowstorm is among the higher joys of Walking, and produces in shortest time the state of ecstasy. Meredith himself has described once for all in *The Egoist* the delight of Walking soaked through by rain. Still more, in mist upon the mountains to keep the way, or to lose and find it, is one of the great primæval games, though now we play it with map and compass. But do not, in mountain mist, "lose the way" on purpose, as I have recommended to vary the monotony of less exciting walks. I once had eight days' walking alone in the Pyrenees, and on only one half-day saw heaven or earth. Yet I enjoyed that week in the mist, for I was kept hard at work finding the unseen way through pine forest and gurgling alp, every bit of instinct and hill knowledge on the stretch. And that one half-day of sunlight, how I treasured it! When we see the mists sweeping up to play with us as we walk the mountain crests we should "rejoice," as it was the custom of Cromwell's soldiers to do when they saw the enemy. Listen while you can to the roar of waters from behind the great grey curtain, and look at the torrent at your feet tumbling the rocks down gully and glen, for there will be no such sights and sounds when the mists are withdrawn into their lairs, and the mountain, no longer a giant half seen through clefts of scudding cloud, stands there, from scree-foot to cairn, dwarfed and betrayed by the sun. So let us "love all changes of weather."

I have now set down my own experiences and likings. Let no one be alarmed or angry because his ideas of Walking are different. There is no orthodoxy in Walking. It is a land of many paths and no-paths, where everyone goes his own way and is right.

# THE MIDDLE MARCHES

" On Keilder-side the wind blaws wide ;
    There sounds nae hunting-horn
That rings sae sweet as the winds that beat
    Round banks where Tyne is born.
The Wansbeck sings with all her springs,
    The bents and braes give ear ;
But the wood that rings wi' the sang she sings
    I may not see nor hear;
For far and far thae blithe burns are,
    And strange is a'thing near."
                    SWINBURNE, *A Jacobite's Exile.*

THE glories of cloudland, the white mountains with their
billowy clefts, lie along the horizon, rather than in the
dome of the sky. They are frescoes on the walls, rather
than on the ceiling, of heaven. Sunrise and sunset often
paint upon them their pictures of an hour, unseen by us,
behind some neighbouring grove or hill. Still more often
do Alpine or Cumbrian mountains, from their very height
and the nearness of one giant to another, hide the wealth
of heaven from the climber on the hillside, who has, however, in those lands his terrestrial compensations. In fen
country the clouds are seen, but at the price of an earth of
flat disillusionment. In Northumberland alone both heaven
and earth are seen; we walk all day on long ridges, high
enough to give far views of moor and valley, and the sense
of solitude above the world below, yet so far distant from
each other, and of such equal height, that we can watch
the low skirting clouds as they " post o'er land and ocean
without rest." It is the land of the far horizons, where
the piled or drifted shapes of gathered vapour are for ever
moving along the farthest ridge of hills, like the procession
of long primæval ages that is written in tribal mounds
and Roman camps and Border towers on the breast of
Northumberland.

# THE MIDDLE MARCHES

The foreground between us and the horizon view is some-times heather, alive with the call and flight of grouse; more often the " bent," as the ballad-writers called the rough white-grass moor, home of sparse broods of black game. The silence is broken only by water's ancient song, as the burn makes its way down rocky hollows towards the hay-makers at work under the sycamore beside the grey-stone farm below. Up above here, on the moor, the silent sheep browse all day long, filling the mind with thoughts of peace and safety; they seem diligent to compensate themselves for a thousand years of raids and interrupted pasture. The farms are so large that often, in spite of good shepherding, the bones of a sheep are found behind some " auld fail dyke "[1]—an old-world landmark of this oozy desert. In the great days the Border poets used to find skeletons, not of sheep only, thus derelict under the wasting wind:

" In behint yon auld fail dyke,
 I wot there lies a new-slain knight;
 And naebody kens that he lies there
 But his hawk, his hound, and his lady fair.

Mony a one for him makes mane,
 But nane sall ken whae he is gane;
 O'er his white banes, when they are bare,
 The wind sall blaw for evermair."

Still the west wind blows over Northumberland, bending seaward each lonely tree. And if it no longer parches the bones of men, around us and under our feet in the covering " bent " are strewn the bones of sheep, and of the lesser victims of the hovering birds of prey. The ungarnished moorland tells no flattering tale. For on it we see written the everlasting alternation of life and death. Peace and beauty reign, but sternly mindful of the conditions of their

---

[1] Fail = turf.

20

tenure, the eternal law that the generations must live by devouring each other. So on the moor:

> " We wot of life through death,
>   How each feeds each we spy."

Northumberland throws over us not a melancholy but a meditative spell:

> " It gives us homeliness in desert air,
>   And sovereignty in spaciousness."

For the distance, the illimitable, is seldom out of sight. The far ridge, the horizon rich with cloud shapes, is always there. Like all the greatest things, like the universe itself, this land does not easily yield up the truth, whether its secret heart is of joy or of sorrow. It heightens both till they are fused, and the dispute between them loses meaning. The great silence is too profound to be broken with a question. The distance is so grand that we cannot wish it near. We are satisfied by we know not what.

One of the greatest of these far views, and the central one of all for the right geographical comprehension of Northumbrian history, is to be had from a ridge two miles south-east of Elsdon, where the Harwood road from the east reaches the summit, pauses appropriately under Winter's Gibbet to take in the western view, and then begins to fall down rapidly to Elsdon and Redesdale. It is markedly a watershed, as will be seen on the map; for it divides the sources of Font and Wansbeck, that flow directly eastward to the sea through the pale of civilization, from the Rede Water and North Tyne Valleys, that here turn and sweep southward for a while through the old lawless borderland, till at last they reach the South Tyne, and turn to flow down with it to Newcastle and the sea. Behind the traveller, as he comes up to the Gibbet, lie a few miles of " bent " and moorland, sloping east towards the agricultural wealth of seaward Northumberland; before him, to the west, suddenly

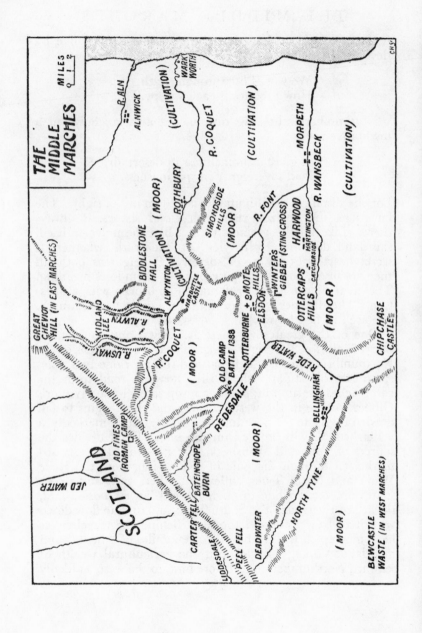

THE MIDDLE MARCHES

MILES
0 1 2

SCOTLAND

JED WATER

GREAT CHEVIOT HILL (IN EAST MARCHES)

KIDLAND LEE
R. USWAY
R. ALWYN

AD FINES (ROMAN CAMP)

CARTER FELL

BATEINGHOPE BURN

LIDDESDALE
PEEL FELL
DEADWATER

NORTH TYNE

BELLINGHAM

(MOOR)

BEWCASTLE WASTE (IN WEST MARCHES)

R. COQUET
(MOOR)
OLD CAMP
BATTLE 1388
OTTERBURNE + o MOTE
REDESDALE
(MOOR)

REDE WATER

ELSDON
WINTER'S GIBBET (STING CROSS)
HARTINGTON
CATCHERSIDE

OTTERCAPS HILLS

HARWOOD

(MOOR)

CHIPCHASE CASTLE

R. FONT

SIMONDSIDE HILLS
(MOOR)

R. COQUET

ALWYNTON
(CULTIVATION)
HARBOTTLE CASTLE

BIDDLESTONE HALL
(MOOR)

ROTHBURY

R. COQUET

(CULTIVATION)

R. ALN
ALNWICK

WARK WORTH

(CULTIVATION)

MORPETH
R. WANSBECK

(CULTIVATION)

CH.S.

revealed as he breasts the ridge, is the Border country—
Redesdale coming down out of the Cheviot Hills in a straight
line for twenty miles, and at its head the massive bluff of
Carter Fell, under whose northern edge the great road
passes into Scotland.

Thus the Gibbet seems the flag of war hung out on the
ramparts by civil against savage man. Yet, in fact, it was
only set up in 1791, when the shepherds of Redesdale and
Tynedale were no longer lawless, but had become honest
Presbyterians, true to the faith of Burns and the Bible. The
corpse of an unheroic tramp named Winter was hanged
here to rot in chains (and finally, when he fell to pieces, in
a sack)—the last case of this legal barbarity perpetuated in
England, they say. He had done a sordid murder in these
parts, which struck such a horror through the law-abiding
North England of that later day that the great Hereford-
shire pugilist, Tom Winter, when he arrived at a national
reputation, had to change his ill-omened name for the
world-renowned title of Tom Spring. The heroic Border
thieves of an earlier age swung for it often at Hexham or
"at that weary Carlisle," or on the numerous "Gallows
Hills" hereabouts; but in their time this spot was marked,
not as now by a wooden gibbet, but by a stone cross, of
which the pedestal still lies sunk in the moss hard by. Sting
Cross, as it was called, stood where its grim successor stands
now, high on the watershed, far seen against the skyline, a
guide and encouragement to the traveller seeking his adventurous way westward on business among the Redesdale
thieves, or bound to pass up their long valley into Scotland.
Sting Cross must have been a landmark well known to the
wagonless armies of the Border, who rode their thirty miles
a day over the moorland. The chivalry of Scotland must have
passed it, on their raids, when they came over "Ottercap
Hills" and "lighted down at Greenleighton." A rough
road now runs by the Gibbet; but then only bridle tracks
crossed the watershed, several probably converging at the
Cross, to fall thence into the marshy bottom of Redesdale.

# THE MIDDLE MARCHES

From the watershed on which the Gibbet stands another and greater watershed is clearly visible, twenty miles away, at the head of Redesdale. This is the curving sweep of the Border Ridge dividing Scotland and England, sweeping down from the north-east to the south-west corner of Northumberland, like the curve of England's head. The view from the Gibbet embraces the north-eastern half of this arc, from the Great Cheviot Hill itself to Carter Fell. There stand the finest of the English Cheviots, ranged round the head-waters of Coquet, Redesdale and North Tyne. This country, the Middle Marches of Border times, once beyond the pale of civilization, is now perhaps the safest and most hospitable district in the whole world, but is still difficult of access, except to the pedestrian, for it lacks roads and inns. In old days there was no road in it along which a wheeled vehicle could pass over the Border. The moss-troopers rode up the length of Redesdale by a track that forded the Rede Water again and again; such, till 1777, was the only way into Scotland through the Middle Marches. Even to-day there are only two roads, one up the North Tyne by Deadwater, and one up the Rede under Carter Fell, ever swarming with tramps and motors. But the tramp who seeks not work but pleasure and meditation penetrates on foot the recesses of these hills and walks along the sharp Border Ridge south-westwards from Great Cheviot, with the Scottish view of the Eildon Hills and Tweed over his right shoulder, and Northumbrian moors over his left. When his high-level walk has led him past the camp where the Romans shivered *ad fines*, and over Carter Fell, he will reach the summit of Peel Fell, where the western view opens before him down Liddesdale to the Solway. In order to avoid leaving the ridge, and going ten miles down-stream in search of the nearest inn, he will gladly seek lodging at night with the Cheviot farmers, true descendants of Dandie Dinmont, hospitable as the Arabs of the desert—Scots and Presbyterians for the most part, even on the English side. These men, assembling from both sides of the Border, still at the

24

New Year hunt the fox in the Bezzle and Henhole, two
rocky gashes on the round sides of Great Cheviot Hill, in
the traditional manner recorded long ago by Scott in the
twenty-fifth chapter of *Guy Mannering*. A run on foot after
the fox, among the moss-hags, on the very top of Great
Cheviot itself, on a frosty morning, with both kingdoms full
in view, is no ill way to begin the year.

Walter Scott, from this encircling Cheviot Ridge, threw
a few lines and phrases at our English streams—Coquet and
Rede picked crumbs from the table he spread for Ettrick
and Teviot and Yarrow. Also he gave us Diana Vernon;
her hunt upon the mountain-side was above Biddlestone
Hall, where the spurs of the English Cheviots, green, round
and steep in that district, overlook the Coquet, as it breaks
from the hills and spreads down over the plain towards
Rothbury.

The English Border was divided for administrative and
military purposes into the East, Middle and West Marches.
The East Marches contained the lands between Berwick
and the great Cheviot Hill—that is, the plain where Till
flows into Tweed and Tweed into the sea, the spacious
Thermopylæ of the war between the two great kingdoms,
studded with famous castles — Etal, Wark, Norham; and
famous battlefields—Homildon Hill and Flodden. This was
one of the two royal routes into Scotland. The East Marches
also included a piece of mountain district, the great Cheviot
Hill and its purlieus, known as the Forest of Cheviot.

The West Marches correspond in general nature to the
East. The plain of Carlisle was the only other route, beside
the plain of Berwick, by which the royal armies with trains
of wagons could be passed over the Border; and there, too,
were famous castles, like Naworth; famous battlefields like
Solway Moss. And the West Marches, like the East, contained a piece of wild country, the Bewcastle and Gilsland
wastes, less mountainous, but more lawless than the Cheviot
Forest.

# THE MIDDLE MARCHES

The East and the West Marches have much the same history. From the beginning of the long wars in the days of Bruce, down to the Union of the Crowns, they were perpetually subject to Scottish invasion. But the plain by the Northern Ocean, and the plain by the Solway Firth, was each inhabited by a well-ordered society, necessarily preoccupied with the military aspects of life, but highly organized by the King's deputies for purposes of internal police and external warfare. Only the Cheviot Forest in the East, and Bewcastle Waste in the West March, shared the geographical and political character of the notorious Middle Marches.

The Middle Marches included Redesdale, North Tynedale, and upper Wansdeck and Coquetdale. Two long reports of Royal Commissioners, one in 1542 and another in 1550, give a minute and fascinating account of the society of these districts towards the close of the long centuries of Border warfare, early in the period celebrated by *The Lay of the Last Minstrel*.[1] The Commissioners tell the King that, in the Middle Marches, the enemy whose raids are most frequent and most formidable is not the Scots, but the English robbers of North Tynedale and Redesdale. The reason is not far to seek. The inhabitants of these two valleys were cut off from the rest of the world, as a glance at the map shows, by the high moorland rampart on which stood Sting Cross; they were thus divided from Coquetdale and Wansbeck, and the plains beyond. They lived secluded, under the influence of perpetual Border warfare, from which the rest of Northumberland was partly sheltered. North Tynedale and Redesdale, as the Commissioners report, are inhabited by a population, sparse according to some standards, but thick out of all proportion to the meagre soil; and as, in North Tynedale at least, very little effort is made at tillage, a great surplus population has to find its subsistence by raiding the country outside the valley bounds.[2]

[1] Hodgson's *Northumberland*, III. ii., pp. 171-248.
[2] Pp. 233, 237-238. The Commission reports 1500 able-bodied men, ready for war and robbery, inhabiting the two valleys.

# THE MIDDLE MARCHES

In Redesdale, although it is reported to have the poorer soil of the two, there is more tillage, and more wealth lawfully acquired. But in both valleys the surplus population lives by raiding the settled country to the east. The raiders were in close league with those of Scottish Liddesdale, where a very similar state of society existed. The national feud was often set aside for the convenience of uniting to prey upon the honest men of the two kingdoms. Thieves, when hard pressed by a foray of the King's officers, could cross the Border at Deadwater and defy extradition.

Indeed the only racial and national allegiance which the warrior of these districts really felt was loyalty towards his own clan. Family feeling served, more than anything else, to protect culprits and defy the law. Stolen property could not be followed up and recovered in the thieving valleys, because each raider was protected by the revengeful jealousy of a large and warlike tribe. The inhabitants of these valleys were grouped in communities based upon the tie of kinship. Small families came for protection under the rule of the Charltons, who answered for half of North Tyne. The Halls, Reeds, Hedleys and Fletchers of Redesdale, the Charltons, Dodds, Robsons and Milbournes of North Tynedale were the real political units within a society that had little other organization. The King, when he raised taxes from these districts, sometimes secured the tribute through the agency of the great families.[1] They united for raids into foreign territory; but they stained their native valley with the blood of intestine feuds. The most famous of these is celebrated in *The Ballad of Percy Reed*, whom the " fausehearted ' Ha's ' " did to death at the famous hunting, high in Bateinghope, under the Carter Fell.[2]

In North Tynedale, more entirely given over to thieving, and less addicted to agriculture than Redesdale, the whole valley wore a barbarous and martial appearance. The

[1] Pp. 229-235 and 243-244, *sub* 1550.
[2] Apparently because Percy Reed had, in an evil hour, allowed himself to be made Royal Keeper of his native valley of Redesdale.

clans lived in strong houses, placed in positions of natural security among the soft deep moss-hags up on the moor, or behind " banks and cleughs of wood wherein of old time for the more strength great trees have been felled and laid so athwart the ways and passages, that in divers places (unless it be by such as know and have experience of those strait and evil ways and passages) it will be hard for strangers having no knowledge thereof to pass thereby in any order and especially on horseback." In this savage and unsettled community, preyed upon by its own feuds, by the Scots and by the English Keeper from Chipchase, the military architects built these " strong houses " not of stone but of great oak beams. (Were there then oak forests in the neighbourhood?) " The outer sides or walls be made of great sware (*sic*) oak trees, strongly bound together with great tenors of the same, so thick mortressed that it will be very hard without great force and labour to break or cast down any of the said houses; the timber as well of the said walls as roofs be so great, and covered most part with turfs and earth that they will not easily burn. In Redesdale the houses were not set in so strong places as they be in Tynedale, nor the passages into them so strait or dangerous." [1]

By the pleasant banks of Coquet another state of society was found. Coquetdale was not, like the two thieving valleys, cut off by any moorland rampart from the rest of Northumberland. Once the river emerges from the hills at Alwynton it flows down through fertile country direct to the sea. Civilization had therefore spread quietly up along the course of its tranquil waters, past Brinkburn and Rothbury, up through the plain of Harbottle, till it reached the foot of the hills. So it is natural that the Commissioners should have to report: " The people of Coquetdale be best prepared for defence, and most defensible people of themselves, and of the truest and best sort of any that do inhabit endlong all the frontier or border of the said Middle Marches of England." But security went no farther up the

---

[1] Hodgson, III. ii., pp. 232-233, 237, *sub* 1542.

stream than Alwynton. The King's peace did not extend to
the sources of the Coquet and its tributaries, the Alwyn
and Usway. These streams come down through the green
Cheviot Hills from the Border Ridge, curving and sweeping
in "great number of hoops and valleys," as the Commissioners say. This ground of Kidland Lee, the most beautiful
part of the English Border, does not, like the wastes round
Rede Water and North Tyne, consist of long, straight ridges,
gradually and slightly raised above valleys several miles
across in prairies of long white rough grass. The Coquet
sources are an exception from this general character of the
Northumbrian scenery; their streams come down through
green rounded hills, cutting for themselves winding passages,
scarcely a hundred yards broad, whose high and slippery
walls, clad in turf and bracken, are too steep for the
pedestrian. He is forced to keep either the valley bottom
or the hill-top; and, if he walks along by the burn bank,
he sees nothing but the steep green wall on each side, and
the blue dome of sky above.

This country was considered to contain "reasonable
good pasture," then as now. But, while now grey-stone
farms are scattered at intervals of a few miles along these
deep valley bottoms, then no one dared live in them, for
fear of the murderous raids of the Scots and the men of
Redesdale. The Commissioners attribute some of these
difficulties to the peculiar nature of the ground:

"The said valleys or hoops of Kydland lie so distant
and divided by mountains one from another, that such as
inhabit in one of these hoops, valleys, or graynes, cannot
hear the fray, outcry, or exclamation of such as dwell in
another hoop or valley upon the other side of the said
mountain, nor come or assemble to their assistance in time
of necessity. Wherefore, we cannot find any of the neigh-
bours thereabouts willing continually to inhabit or plenish
within the said ground of Kydland, and especially in winter
time; although they might have stone houses builded
thereupon for their defence, and also have the said ground

free without paying rent for the same. The dangers afore recited be so great and manifest." [1]

In the summer time, indeed, the law-abiding men of Coquetdale drove their flocks afield up these higher valleys, and lived out in " sheals," watching them. This practice, then common in Northumberland, of " shealing " or " summering," analogous to the high summer pasturage of Alpine districts,[2] was, however, impossible round the head-waters of Coquet and Usway in time of " war or troublous peace." So, in time of war with Scotland, or in years when the men of Redesdale were in an evil humour, no bleating of sheep was heard all the summer long amid the winding passages of the hills; and the black-cock strutted through the bracken on the steep bank above, and the heron fished beside the sparkling stream, month after month, undisturbed by man, save when now and again a hungry spearman rode swiftly and silently through the silent land. In happier days to come these steep, slippery banks of Alwyn and Usway were hunted by Diana and the Osbaldistone pack; and these passages of the hills were threaded by Andrew Fairservice and his friends the smugglers, and his enemies the Jacobites.

A few miles below the place where Coquet and its tributaries at length break out into the plain stand the ruins of Harbottle Castle, on a green hill by the river. It was from this comparatively well-ordered and secure district that the short arm of the King was occasionally extended into Redesdale. Harbottle Castle was the headquarters of the Keeper of Redesdale; he dared live no nearer to the valley of which he had charge, for fear of the fate that befell Percy Reed. The Commissioners of 1542 advised that if thirty horsemen were kept in Harbottle Castle, ever ready to mount and ride behind the Keeper over the steep Elsdon Hill into

[1] Hodgson, III. ii., p. 223.
[2] " There is a martiall kinde of men which lie out, up and downe in little cottages, called by them sheals and shealings, from Aprill to August, in a scattering fashion, summering, as they term it, their cattle " (Speed's *Great Britaine*, 1611, *sub* Northumberland).

Redesdale, that turbulent valley might be kept in order. At Chipchase fifty mounted men would be required for like service by the Keeper of North Tynedale. Meanwhile, stones and mortar were as much required as men and horses: Harbottle Castle had "for lack of necessary reparations fallen into extreme ruin and decay." [1]

But, since the impoverished State could not afford to take these necessary measures to extend its control into the two thieving valleys, it attempted to isolate them by an elaborate system of local watch and ward. The farmers and gentlemen bordering along the lower reaches of Rede Water and North Tyne were expected to keep nightly watch at their own expense, to prevent the thieves from passing down towards the coast, or into the civilized valleys of Coquet and Wansbeck. A watch is "to be surely kept upon the night time, that is to say, from the sunset until the sunrise at diverse places, passages, and fords, endlong all the said Middle Marches, for the better preservation of the same from thieves and spoils." Henry VIII.'s Commissioners presented him with a list of the places where two horsemen are supposed to be stationed every night. Roughly, the line runs along the watershed on the top of which the Sting Cross was so prominent a feature. The charge of maintaining the watchmen was laid on the men of this district. The "townships" (some, like Harrington, Greenleighton, Catcherside, scarcely more than a group of farm-buildings), standing in lonely places along the eastern slope of the watershed, had to maintain the nightly guard for the protection of the rich seaward districts. Naturally, complaint and recrimination arose, and the Commissioners of 1542 were faced by an interesting problem of the proper incidence of local rates. The Borderers of the hill townships complained that all the expense of the ward fell on them, and the advantage to the low country. The men of the low

---

[1] This was in 1542. In 1550 it had been partly repaired, but had still no hall, kitchen or brewhouse, or enough room for prisoners (Hodgson, III. ii., pp. 212, 237, 243.)

country replied that the watch was so ill kept that they themselves had to maintain night watches in their seaward townships against the frequent invasions of the men of Redesdale and North Tyne.[1] We may well believe that the thieves found it no hard matter to ride eastward through the line at night, avoiding each of the widely scattered points where, as all the world knew, two shivering watchmen were eagerly hoping that the day would dawn before they had met with any unpleasant encounter. The difficulty of the thieves in effecting their return journey with large droves of cattle would no doubt be more severe; and it was perhaps at this latter part of the "fray" that the watchmen were expected to make themselves most useful.

The first social and political duty of the English and Scottish Borderer was to "follow the fray" — that is, to mount at a moment's notice and ride in pursuit of plunderers. As the "riding" ballads, such as *Jamie Telfer*, show, personal affection was not always strong enough to induce the farmer, awakened in the small hours of the morning, to turn out and endanger his life on behalf of a neighbour who had "brought him the fray":

> " The sun was na up, but the moon was down,
>     It was the gryming o' a new fa'n snaw,
> Jamie Telfer has run three myles a-foot,
>     Between the Dodhead and the Stob's Ha'.
>
> And when he cam to the fair tower gett,
>     He shouted aloud, and cried weel hie,
> Till out bespak auld Tibby Elliot—
>     ' Wha's this that brings the fraye to me? '
>
> ' It's I, Jamie Telfer o' the fair Dodhead,
>     And a harried man I think I be!
> There's naething left at the fair Dodhead
>     But a waefu' wife and bairnies three.'

---

[1] Hodgson, III. ii., pp. 238-242.

# THE MIDDLE MARCHES

' Gae seek you succour at Branksome Ha',
    For succour ye'se get nane frae me;
Gae seek your succour where ye paid blackmail,
    For, man! ye ne'er paid money to me.' "

The scene of this suggestive dialogue is laid in Scotland;
but there must often have been the same story to tell in
Northumberland. The repeated efforts of the Tudor
Government to make the duty of "following the fray" a
State obligation, enforceable by fine, were, in the end, largely
successful, though even towards the close of Elizabeth's
reign the average of murders on the English side was
estimated at over a hundred, and the average of property
stolen at over £10,000 in a year.[1]

But all this talk of "thieves" is beside the point which
gives value to the history of the Borderland. What is it
that has brought our cultured and commercial society to
collect the relics of these cut-throats? If we ascribe it all
to Scott, why did he make them his stock-in-trade? It is not
that the moss-troopers can claim any monopoly in robbery
and murder. There is a murder every night in our evening
papers; and our thefts are too plentiful to bear recording.
If, again, it is armed lawlessness and cruelty that we want,
or the primitive social state, we can find these in the history
of any barbarous people; and if we want them in a setting
of mountain scenery, there are the Balkans to our hand
to-day. What, then, was peculiar to the Border life which
Scott celebrated? It was this: that the Border people wrote
the Border Ballads. Like the Homeric Greeks, they were
cruel, coarse savages, slaying each other as the beasts of the
forest; and yet they were also poets who could express in
the grand style the inexorable fate of the individual man
and woman, and infinite pity for all the cruel things which
they none the less perpetually inflicted upon one another.
It was not one ballad-maker alone, but the whole cut-throat

[1] Creighton, *Historical Essays*, " The Northumbrian Border," pp. 256,
263-265.

# THE MIDDLE MARCHES

population who felt this magnanimous sorrow, and the consoling charm of the highest poetry. A large body of popular ballads commemorated real incidents of this wild life, or adapted folk-lore stories to the places and conditions of the Border. The songs so constructed on both sides of the Cheviot Ridge were handed down by oral tradition among the shepherds, and among the farm-girls who, for centuries, sang them to each other at the milking. If the people had not loved the songs many of the best would have perished. The Border Ballads, for good and for evil, express this society and its quality of mind as well and truly as the daily Press and the music-hall stage express that of the majority of the town-dwellers of to-day.

The Border Ballads are distinguished from the old ballads of South England, similar in form and often based upon the same folk-legends, by a tenser poetic strain and a deeper melancholy. Their more tragic mood may be in some part due to the real conditions of life prevailing in the Border country, where violent death dogged man's footsteps every day. To be a lover in a South English ballad is to run a fair chance of " living happily ever afterwards "; but to assume the part in a Border Ballad is a desperate undertaking. No father, mother, brother or rival will have pity before it is too late; they are " more fanged than wolves and bears." And chance is generally in league with the Tragic Muse. When her brother determines to burn Lady Maisry for loving an Englishman too well, Lord William rides up just too late to do anything but burn her whole family in revenge. Even when the ballad ends well there has generally been blood shed, as in the original *Lochinvar*, which has none of the rollicking canter and swagger of Scott's modern rendering.[1] And the best ballads are the most tragic. Something grand and inevitable, like the doom impending over the Lion Gate at Mycenæ, broods over each of these stone peel-towers high upon the " bent," and rude forts of " great sware oak trees," " covered with turfs." Even

[1] *Katherine Janfarie.* (Aytoun's *Ballads*, 1858, ii., p. 75.)

34

the most wicked and horrible stories are not sordid, but
tragic:

> " ' Why does your brand sae drop wi' blude,
>         Edward, Edward?
>   Why does your brand sae drop wi' blude,
>         And why sae sad gang ye, O? '

.    .    .    .    .    .    .

> ' O I hae killed my father dear,
>         Mither, mither;
>   O I hae killed my father, dear,
>         Alas! and wae is me, O! '

.    .    .    .    .    .    .

> ' And what will ye do wi' your tow'rs and your ha',
>         Edward, Edward?
>   And what will ye do wi' your tow'rs and your ha',
>         That were sae fair to see, O? '

> ' I'll let them stand till they doun fa',
>         Mither, mither;
>   I'll let them stand till they doun fa',
>         For here never mair maun I be, O.' "

Or, again, when Helen of Kirkconnell has been killed by
a shot aimed at her lover, not even a fierce revenge can
give him any ease:

> " As I went down the water side,
>   None but my foe to be my guide,
>   None but my foe to be my guide,
>         On fair Kirkconnell Lee.
>
>   I lighted down, my sword did draw,
>   I hack'd him into pieces sma',
>   I hack'd him into pieces sma',
>         For her sake that died for me.
>
>   I wish I were where Helen lies!
>   Night and day on me she cries,
>   And I am weary of the skies,
>         For her sake that died for me."

*Lyke-Wake Dirge* is perhaps the most awful and solemn expression that was ever given to the barbarous popular religion of the Dark Ages, as distinct from the higher flights of more cultivated Italian and French Catholicism. Yet in nine Border Ballads out of ten there is no religious *motif*; and consolation is hardly ever sought in expectation of a meeting in heaven. The sense of human life, its passions, its love, its almost invariable tragedy, seem the abiding thoughts of this savage but great-souled people. The supernatural world consists of ghosts of the departed, and of the fairies—those friends with whom the poets go on mysterious rides like that of *Thomas the Rhymer*:

" O they rad on, and farther on,
　　And they waded through rivers aboon the knee,
And they saw neither sun nor moon,
　　But they heard the roaring of the sea.

It was mirk, mirk night, and there was nae stern [1] light,
　　And they waded thro' red blude to the knee,
For a' the blude that's shed on earth
　　Rins through the springs o' that countrie."

In another ballad the Queen of Fairies steals a young mother from a farm to be *Elphin Nourice* (elf nurse) to the little Prince of Fairies. The poor woman hears out of fairyland a noise of the dear world she has left, and remembers her own son:

" ' I heard a cow low, a bonnie cow low,
　　An' a cow low doun in yon glen;
Lang, lang, will my young son greet,
　　Or his mither bid him come ben.

' I heard a cow low, a bonnie cow low,
　　An' a cow low doun in yon fauld;
Lang, lang, will my young son greet,
　　Or his mother take him frae cauld.

[1] Stern=star.

36

' Waken, Queen of Elfan,
    An' hear your Nourice moan.'

' O moan ye for your meat,
    Or moan ye for your fee,
Or moan ye for the ither bounties
    That ladies are wont to gie? '

' I moan na for my meat,
    Nor yet for my fee,
But I mourn for Christen land—
    It's there I fain would be.' "

The Border Life, at any rate in its most highly developed
form in the thieving valleys, had no set object, no political
or social end to attain. It was a life good or bad in itself
alone. These people have left nothing behind except these
ballads, which have made all their meaningless and wicked
ways interesting for all time. Law-making, road-laying,
bridge-building—everything which Carlyle would have approved—had no place in their ambitions. Their life was a
game with Death, in which each in turn was sure soon to
pay forfeit; it was played according to certain rules of family
honour, varied and crossed by lovers' passions. All classes
of a sparse population joined in this game with Death, and
relished it as the poetry and breath of life. It is useless to
wish the conditions of that life back in the hope of getting
ballads instead of music-hall songs; men often drive away
cattle without writing immortal poetry, and to drive cattle
and leave the owner dead on his hearthstone is in itself a
very bad thing.

The inhabitants of the Cheviot Hills to-day are a fine
people, and, upon the whole, greatly preferable to the moss-
troopers. Burns and the Bible long ago superseded the
Ballads; and vulgarity has not yet invaded from the cities.
In the course of the last three centuries the Scottish farmers
have moved into and occupied the English Cheviot valleys.

The origin of this movement is said to have been the persecution in the "killing times" of Claverhouse, when a Covenanter had a better chance of safety on the English side of the Border. But the movement has not yet come to an end; and it is difficult to say how far the inhabitants of Redesdale are descendants of the Englishmen of the sixteenth century, and how far of Scottish immigrants.

The social and religious state of the valley half-way between the Border times and our own is described in a most amusing letter written from the fine old peel-tower of Elsdon, then, as now, used as the Rectory, where the unfortunate incumbent, Mr Dodgson, had been snowed up. He is the best type of an eighteenth-century clergyman and letter-writer, a worthy contemporary of Sterne and Horace Walpole. Of course it has never entered his head that moorland scenery is anything but a horror.[1]

"There is not a town in all the parish, except Elsdon itself be called one; the farmhouses, where the principal families live, are five or six miles distant from one another; and the whole country looks like a desert. The greater part of the richest farmers are Scotch dissenters, and go to a meeting-house at Birdhope Craig, about ten miles from Elsdon; however, they don't interfere in ecclesiastical matters, or study polemical divinity. Their religion descends from father to son, and is rather a part of the personal estate than the result of reasoning, or the effect of enthusiasm. Those who live near Elsdon come to the church, those at a greater distance towards the west go to the meeting-house at Birdhope Craig; others, both Churchmen and Presbyterians, at a very great distance, go to the nearest church or conventicle in the neighbouring parish. There is a very good understanding between the parties; for they not only intermarry with each other, but frequently do penance together in a white sheet with a white wand, barefoot, in one of the coldest churches in England, and at the coldest seasons of the year. I dare not finish the description for

[1] *Northumberland Table Book* (Legendary Division), vol. i., p. 232.

fear of bringing on a fit of the ague; indeed, the ideas of sensation are sufficient to starve a man to death without having recourse to those of reflection. If I was not assured by the best authority upon earth that the world was to be destroyed by fire, I should conclude that the day of destruction is at hand, and brought on by means of an agent very opposite to that of heat. There is not a single tree or hedgerow within twelve miles to break the force of the wind; it sweeps down like a deluge from hills capped with everlasting snow, and blasts almost the whole country into one continued barren desert. The whole country is doing penance in a white sheet; for it began to snow on Sunday night, and the storm has continued ever since."

Yet, for all this, Elsdon lays firm hold on the imagination of those who are not intimidated by moorland scenery, and who love the Northumbrian ridges. It remains to-day as the spiritual capital of the Middle Marches, the yet unviolated shrine of the tradition of the English Border. It served the Redesdale clans for their common place of burial and of religious rites, their market and assembly place, as Bellingham served the men of North Tynedale. But whereas Bellingham has now a railway, and has suffered change, Elsdon is the same as ever. It lies low in a green hollow, visible from many surrounding heights; and one glance at it from far off recalls the life of innumerable generations. The famous Mote Hills, green mound-circles towering above the burn, tell that Elsdon was the capital of Redesdale in days when neither Scotland nor England existed. The church, beneath which lie the dead of Otterburn, and the peel-tower thrusting up through the scant trees its battlements and its stone roof, call back the Border life, while the stone houses scattered round the broad village green mark the civilizing progress of the eighteenth century.

Otterburn, the glorified Border foray of 1388, was fought a few miles higher up the Rede valley. It was there that they " bickered on the bent." The Douglas himself had come over the Border with an army of picked men, burnt

Northumberland and Durham, and had, before the closed gates of Newcastle, given Harry Percy a challenge to follow and fight him before he recrossed the Border. It was chivalry and love of the game, and no military considerations, that made Douglas wait for Percy; he occupied an old tribal entrenchment, still clearly traceable on a knoll above Greenchesters, beyond Otterburn. It was chivalry that made Hotspur attack the camp at nightfall, when his English bowmen could not show their skill, when all his men were wearied with a forced march of thirty miles that day from Newcastle, when reinforcements under the Bishop of Durham were scarcely twelve hours behind.[1] The result was the midnight battle of heroes, ending in an English rout. Douglas was killed; but Hotspur was taken, and the remainder of his men fled back past Elsdon, hotly pursued, but often turning fiercely on their pursuers. As the August day dawned they were struggling up the side of the high ridges, to south and east of Elsdon, in broken parties of wounded and wearied men. Some of the fliers and pursuers were met by the Bishop of Durham's forces, who had marched hard over the moors and streams by the light of that moon which was glinting on the flash of swords at Otterburn.

The skeletons of a regiment of men, mostly in the prime of life, many of them with skulls cleft, have been found under Elsdon Church, and are believed to be the English killed on that famous night. The main part of the aisle was built about that date, perhaps in memorial of them. But at the western end there still stand two massive Norman pillars, black and dripping with age; beneath them, we may fairly suppose, were laid out the long lines of the dead, brought there on the

" biers
Of birch and hazel grey,"

[1] A good authority on the locality, time and circumstances of the battle is Robert White's *Battle of Otterburn*, 1857.

which the mourners had hastily torn from the clefts of the burns that empty themselves into the Rede. And there is preserved in the church a slab of time-blackened stone, whereon is carved, in rude and barbarous fashion, a nameless knight in the armour of that time. The church is the tomb of the old Border life; and the hills around are the everlasting monument. One form of life has passed away; but another has come to take its place. As we climb the steep green road again towards the Gibbet at Sting Cross we see the clouds still moving along the far horizon ridges; the sun sets over Carter Fell; the stars come out against the blackness:

" Life glistens on the river of the death."

# JOHN WOOLMAN, THE QUAKER

THERE are three religious autobiographies that I think of together—the *Confessions* of St Augustine and of Rousseau and the *Journal* of John Woolman, the Quaker. Each of these men had soul-life abundantly, and the power of recording his experiences in that kind; and each gave the impulse to a great current in the world's affairs—the Mediæval Church, the French Revolution, and the Anti-Slavery Movement. But Woolman is to me the most attractive, and I am proud to think that it was he who was the Anglo-Saxon—the " woolman " of old English trader stock.

There is an element of self in the finest ecstasies of St Augustine, the spiritual parent of *Johannes Agricola in Meditation* as depicted by Robert Browning, and of all that hard soul-saving clan. He begins religion at the opposite end from Francis of Assisi, and they never meet. The African saint started Western Europe on the downward course of religious persecution proper. Before him there had, indeed, been persecution of religions for racial or political reasons, but St Augustine was perhaps the chief of those who supplied the religious motive for religious persecution, and turned God Himself into Moloch, a feat which no one but a really " good " man could have performed. Thenceforth, until the age of the much-abused Whigs and sceptics, all the best people in the world were engaged in torturing each other and making earth into hell. It was through St Augustine rather than through Constantine that the Church drank poison. The torch was handed down from him through St Dominic and St Ignatius till it scorched the hand of St John of Geneva by the pyre of Servetus. They were all, at least after their conversions, unusually " good " men, but not good all through like John Woolman.

Rousseau, at any rate, was not " good." We all ought to read his *Confessions*, but I fear the reason why many of us perform this duty is not always the highest. For this great spiritual reformer owns up to common weaknesses indulged to degrees that rise to an epic height. The story of the piece of ribbon thrills us with a moment's illusion that we are morally superior to the man who started the " religious reaction " and the love of mountains, as well as the French Revolution. And then he fulfilled the social contract by leaving his babies at the door of the foundling hospital. The imaginary story of the youth and manhood of one of those unfathered children of genius, say during the French Revolution, would be a fine theme for an historical fictionist of imagination and humour : Stevenson, for instance, would have loved to show by what strange routes through the Quartier Latin or elsewhere that deserted brood of the " old Serpent of Eternity " found their way to the Morgue—or perhaps to a bourgeois' easy-chair. O " Savoyard Vicar," first lover of the mountains, brother of the poor, shaker down of empires, how from such weakness as yours was born such strength? No wonder he puzzles his biographers, of whom himself was the first. No one can understand those who do not understand themselves.

Rousseau, having puzzled himself, inevitably puzzled Lord Morley, who had caught hold of simple Voltaire and packed him neatly into one small volume (with Frederick thrown in, to keep him company), while the insoluble problem of Rousseau trails on through two volumes—the more interesting but the less " final " of the twin biographies. Carlyle, though he posed Rousseau for " Hero as man of letters," did not even touch the problem. But the uncouth, rebellious child of nature struck in him sympathetic chords, and evoked outbursts of grim Carylean humour, thus :

" He could be cooped into garrets, laughed at as a maniac, left to starve like a wild beast in his cage ;—but he could not be hindered from setting the world on fire. His semi-delirious speculations on the miseries of civilized life, and suchlike, helped well to produce a whole delirium in France generally. True, you may well ask,—what could the world, the governors

of the world, do with such a man? Difficult to say what the
governors of the world could do with him! What he could
do with them is unhappily clear enough,—*guillotine* a great
many of them!"

On another occasion, it is said, at a very English dinner-
table, Carlyle was bored by a tribe of Philistines who were
reiterating over their port our great insular doctrine that
"political theories make no difference to practice." After
listening long in silence he growled out: "There was once
a man called Rousseau. He printed a book of political
theories, and the nobles of that land laughed. But the next
edition was bound in their skins." And so, with a Scottish
peasant's big chuckle, he fell silent again amid the apologetic
coughs of the discomposed dinner-party.

John Woolman was a contemporary of Voltaire and
Rousseau though he scarcely knew it. And the spirit of
that age, "dreaming on things to come," spoke a new
word through him also, bidding men prepare the ground
for what we may call the Anglo-Saxon Revolution, the
abolition of negro slavery. Woolman's *Journal* tells how
this humblest and quietest of men used to travel round on
foot, year after year, among these old-fashioned American
Quakers, stirring their honest but sleepy consciences on this
new point of his touching "the holding their fellow-men as
property." A Quaker Socrates, with his searching, simple
questions, he surpassed his Athenian prototype in love and
patience and argumentative fairness, as much as he fell
below him in intellect. And when the Friends found that
they could not answer John's questions, instead of poisoning
him or locking him up as an anarchist, they let their slaves
go free! Truly, a most surprising outcome for the colloquy
of wealthy and settled men with a humble and solitary
pedestrian! Incredible as it may seem, they asked no one
for "Compensation"! But then the Quakers always were
an odd people.

Woolman's religious experience, from first to last, con-

# JOHN WOOLMAN, THE QUAKER

cerned his love and duty toward his fellow-creatures, and
not the selfish salvation of his own soul. His conversion, we
may say, dated from the following incident in his childhood:

"On going to a neighbour's house, I saw on the way a
robin [1] sitting on her nest, and as I came near she went off;
but having young ones, she flew about and with many cries
expressed her concern for them. I stood and threw stones
at her, and one striking her she fell down dead. At first I
was pleased with the exploit, but after a few minutes was
seized with horror at having, in a sportive way, killed an
innocent creature while she was careful for her young. I
beheld her lying dead, and thought those young ones, for
which she was so careful, must now perish for want of their
dam to nourish them. After some painful considerations on
the subject, I climbed up the tree, took all the young birds
and killed them, supposing that better than to leave them
to pine away and die miserably. In this case I believed that
Scripture proverb was fulfilled, *The tender mercies of the
wicked are cruel.* I then went on my errand, and for some
hours could think of little else but the cruelties I had committed, and was much troubled. Thus He whose tender
mercies are over all His works hath placed a principle in
the human mind, which incites to exercise goodness towards
every living creature."

He was so filled with the spirit of love that he became,
as it were, unconscious of danger and suffering when he
was about the work dictated by this impelling force.

"Twelfth of sixth month," 1763, in time of war with the
Red Indians, "being the first of the week and a rainy day,
we continued in our tent, and I was led to think on the
nature of the exercise which hath attended me. Love was
the first motion, and thence a concern arose to spend some
time with the Indians, that I might feel and understand
their life and the spirit they live in, if haply I might receive
some instruction from them, or they might be in any degree helped forward by my following the leadings of truth

[1] The American, not the English, robin.

among them; and as it pleased the Lord to make way for my going at a time when the troubles of war were increasing, and when by reason of much wet weather travelling was more difficult than usual at that season, I looked upon it as a more favourable opportunity to season my mind, and to bring me into a nearer sympathy with them." And so he went among the Indians to exchange with them what we should now call "varieties of religious experience," at a time when one section of them had proclaimed "war with the English," and were actually bringing back English scalps.

His objections to luxury, which he carried to the greatest lengths in his own case, were based not on any ascetic feeling, but on the belief that luxury among the well-to-do was a cause of their rapacity and therefore of their oppression of the poor. "Expensive living," he writes, "hath called for a large supply, and in answering this call the faces of the poor have been ground away and made thin through hard dealing." He was himself a man of but slender means, yet on this ground he denied himself things which he regarded as luxuries, and others would call common comforts. Humanity he thought of as a whole, not as a collection of individuals each busy saving his own soul or amassing his own fortune. The rich, he held, were responsible for the miseries of the poor, and the " good " for the sins of the reprobate. "The law of Christ," he said, "consisted in tenderness towards our fellow-creatures, and a concern so to walk that our conduct may not be the means of strengthening them in error."

If the world could take John Woolman for an example in religion and politics instead of St Augustine and Rousseau we should be doing better than we are in the solution of the problems of our own day. Our modern conscience-prickers often are either too " clever " or too violent. What they have said in one play or novel they must contradict in the next for fear of appearing simple. Or if they are frankly simple, they will set fire to your house to make you listen to their argument. " Get the writings of John Woolman by heart," said Charles Lamb—sound advice not only for lovers of good books but for would-be reformers.

They say John Brown in the ghost went marching along in front of the Northern armies. Then I guess John Woolman was bringing up the ambulance behind. He may have lent a spiritual hand to Walt Whitman in the flesh, bandaging up those poor fellows. As to John Brown, to use a Balkan expression, he was a *comitadji*, " undaunted, true and brave." He could knock up families at night and lead out the fathers and husbands to instant execution, or be hung himself, with an equal sense of duty done, all in the name of the Lord, who he reckoned was antagonistic to negro slavery. And then came the war, those slaughterings by scores of thousands of the finest youthful manhood in the world, the grinding up of the seed-corn of Anglo-Saxon America, from which racially she can never wholly recover. And all because the majority of slave-owners, not being Quakers, had refused to listen to John Woolman. Close your ears to John Woolman one century and you will get John Brown the next, with Grant to follow.

The slave-owners in the British Empire were not Quakers, but fortunately for us they were a feeble folk, few enough to be bought out quietly. One of England's characteristic inventions is Revolution by purchase. It saves much trouble, but it is a luxury that only rich societies can afford. It was lucky for England that George III. did not keep the Southern colonies when he lost us New England. It very nearly happened so, and if it had, then would Old England have been wedded to slavery. As it is she became John Woolman's best pupil.

The Anti-Slavery movement was quite as important as the French Revolution. For if the " industrial revolution " had been fully developed, all the world over, while men still thought it right to treat black men as machines, the exploitation of the tropics by the modern company-promoter on " Congo " lines would have become the rule instead

47

of the exception. Central America, Africa, perhaps India and ultimately China, would be one hell, and Europe would be corrupted as surely as old Rome when she used the conquered world as a stud-farm to breed slaves for her *latifundia*. The Anti-Slavery movement came in the nick of time, just before machinery could universalize the slave system. Slavery on the scale of our modern industries, binding all the continents together in one wicked system of exploitation, would have been too big an "interest" for reformers to tackle. Even as it was, America was very nearly strangled by "cotton" in the Southern States, a more evil and a far more formidable thing than the old eighteenth-century domestic slavery in the same region. But Wilberforce had by that time set the main current of the world's opinion the other way. So it was too late. But how would it have gone with the world if that poor Quaker clerk had kept to himself those first queer questionings of his about "holding fellow-men as property"? Woolman was not a bigwig in his own day, and he will never be a bigwig in history. But if there be a "perfect witness of all-judging Jove," he may expect his meed of much fame in heaven. And if there be no such witness we need not concern ourselves. He was not working for "fame" either here or there.

# JOHN BUNYAN [1]

" As I walked through the wilderness of this world, I lighted on a certain place, where was a Den, and I laid me down in that place to sleep. And as I slept, I dreamed a dream. I dreamed, and behold *I saw a Man clothed with rags, standing in a certain place, with his face from his own house, a Book in his hand, and a great Burden upon his back.* I looked, and saw him open the Book, and read therein; and as he read, he wept and trembled; and not being able longer to contain, he broke out with a lamentable cry, saying ' *What shall I do?* ' "

Of all the works of high imagination which have enthralled mankind, none opens with a passage that more instantly places the reader in the heart of all the action that is to follow; not Homer's, not Milton's, invocation of the Muse; not one of Dante's three great openings; not the murmured challenge of the sentinels on the midnight platform at Elsinore—not one of these better performs the author's initial task. The attention is at once captured, the imagination aroused. In these first sentences, by the magic of words, we are transported into a world of spiritual values, and impressed at the very outset with the sense of great issues at stake—nothing less than the fate of a man's soul.

Without prelude we find ourselves standing in the very centre of the business. Already we breathe the allegoric yet intensely human atmosphere of the book which, for all its power of vision, differs from the figurative poetry of Spenser and Shelley in being firmly planted in the real facts of human nature, and in the real social and economic surroundings of seventeenth-century England.

For the author of *Pilgrim's Progress* was not only a great writer and a powerful religious teacher; he was also an

---

[1] A Commemorative Address delivered at Cambridge in the year 1928, being the three hundredth after John Bunyan's birth.

Englishman who had mixed in all the common traffic of humanity — war, trade, marriage and fatherhood — who shrewdly observed his fellow-men and women, and was by no means devoid of humour. And so—as literary authorities tell us — he founded the English novel, though such was not his design as author, but only to win for Christ poor souls lost in the dark, as he himself had once been lost.

The people who talk about "art for art's sake" and "the distracting influence of a moral purpose in art" have never yet produced art on a par with Milton's or Bunyan's, and they never will. The greatest artists are even more interested in life than in art. Art seems to them a something given, by which to interpret the significance of life.

Bunyan was not a mere religious enthusiast; he was, however unconsciously, an artist as well. When he wrote *Pilgrim's Progress* the first fierce paroxysm of his religious experience had waned, leaving him free to employ his art in recording his past tribulations. If poetry is, as has been said, "emotion recollected in tranquillity," no wonder *Pilgrim's Progress* is a great poem. The man who had believed for a year on end that he had committed the unpardonable sin, had some emotion to recollect. " I can remember," writes Bunyan, " I can remember my fears and doubts and sad months, with comfort. They are as the head of Goliath in my hand."

Now all this stands clearly out in these first pregnant sentences of the book. The first words clearly show us Bunyan in his two aspects, as the author and as the subject of the book; the dreamer who is himself the dream. First we are told of the author: " As I walked through the wilderness of this world, I lighted on a certain place, where was a Den, and I laid me down in that place to sleep. And as I slept I dreamed a dream." And in the very next words we are shown Bunyan as the Pilgrim himself, of whom the tale is told. " I dreamed, and behold I saw a Man."

The dreamer and dream are one and the same man, but

at two different stages of his life's pilgrimage. The dreamer (which is, being interpreted, the author) can afford to exercise his art in tranquillity, for he has arrived safe in a spiritual haven—none the less if the material surrounding thereof be Bedford Jail. Thence he looks back at his former self, the man who stood in solitary places with a Book in his hand, crying lamentably, "What shall I do?" That lonely, tragic figure is the Bunyan whom we know in *Grace Abounding*, the wonderful autobiography that we may regard as the raw material of the yet more wonderful allegory.

But that lonely figure, with the book and the burden and the lamentable cry, is not only Bunyan himself. It is also the representative Puritan of the English Puritan epoch, that epoch of which Bunyan was the most faithful mirror in literature, as Cromwell in action. When Bunyan was a young man, in the years that followed Naseby, Puritanism had come to its moment of greatest force and vigour, in war, in politics, in literature and in all aspects of national life. But the inner pulse of the machine that drove all that tremendous energy of construction and destruction " posting o'er land and ocean without rest," with consequences famous and notorious to all time; the prime motive force of it all was just this lonely figure of the man in the first paragraph of the *Pilgrim's Progress*—the poor man seeking salvation with tears, with no guide save the Bible in his hand. To the poor also the gospel was preached, and, what is stranger, *by* the poor also was it preached. Multiply by tens of thousands that " Man clothed with rags, with . . . a Book in his hand, and a great Burden upon his back," and you have a force of tremendous potency, which has been one of the chief elements in the growth of modern England; the force by means of which Oliver Cromwell and George Fox and John Wesley wrought their wonders, being men of a like experience themselves; the force by alliance with which the more sceptical Whig aristocracy long bore rule in the island, and therewith balanced other forces, in that equipoise

# JOHN BUNYAN

of freedom that has made modern England. During Bunyan's youth this force of Puritan enthusiasm was running like lava burst from the pent volcano's side over the whole land, overwhelming churches and lordships and kings. Later, after the Restoration, came a period of repression and reprisal, from which Bunyan in the prime of life was one of the chief sufferers. And finally, after the Revolution of 1688, the year Bunyan died, Puritanism found its assigned place in the life of England, was harnessed serviceably to the uses of the commonweal, and, whether as Nonconformity or as Evangelicalism in the pale of the Established Church, gave a tone to the domestic and commercial and philanthropic life of modern England. It was this same force of Puritanism that, in the world of imaginative creation, inspired the sterner half of Milton's genius, and all of John Bunyan's genius except that part of him which was pure human.

Ever since the time of Wycliffe, the "Man clothed with rags, with . . . a Book in his hand, and a great Burden upon his back," had been an element in the religious life of England. It was a native element in our national life, not imported from abroad, but begun by Wycliffe's Lollards; their Bible-reading is one of the scenes very rightly chosen to represent English history in the new cartoons in the House of Commons lobby.

But this element of popular Protestantism grew slowly, though steadily. In Tudor times it did not sweep England as it swept Scotland under John Knox. The Reformation that broke the bonds of Rome was effected in part by other forces—the anti-clericalism of a people tired of the predominance of priests, but not yet converted to a new religion; the greed of kings and courtiers; the pride of a nation no longer content to be governed from Italy or Spain. In Tudor times popular Protestantism was only one of the elements that made the Reformation, though it was the most essential element of all; it stemmed the reaction of Mary's reign, and made the Protestant tradition of the

# JOHN BUNYAN

island, by enduring those terrible martyrdoms. It was not
the gentry or the spoilers of the monasteries, but clergy
and cobblers and other poor men who were found ready to
die at the stake by hundreds. In Elizabeth's reign, this
popular Protestantism, sheltered within certain limits by
the new national Church and State, grew apace. But it
was only the attempt of Laud to drive it out of the country
or suppress it altogether that caused that memorable ex-
plosion of its latent forces in the midst of which Bunyan
passed his youth.

Laud tried to enforce a principle that still has many to
advocate it but no longer any to enforce it. Laud's principle
was that the poor, being ignorant, should take their religion
from the learned. But there are other elements in religion
besides learning and tradition. There are the instincts of
a man's own heart and soul, be he learned like Laud, or be
his learning confined, like Bunyan's, almost to the Bible
and Foxe's *Book of Martyrs,* and Luther's *Commentary on
Galatians.* The answer to Laud's thesis was not the axe of
the men who killed him in base revenge: the true con-
futation of Laud's contempt for unlearned religion lay in
the lives and works of John Bunyan and George Fox. If
the battle of Naseby had gone the other way, Laud's followers would have suppressed the future activities of young
Bunyan and young Fox. We should have had no *Pilgrim's
Progress* and no Quakers. Both Bunyan and Fox were
products of that rapid seed-time and harvest of religious
experiment that intervened between the battle of Naseby
and the Restoration.

But this " freedom of prophesying," for which Cromwell
and his Cambridgeshire Ironsides used their swords so well,
had other enemies besides Laud. The orthodox Presbyterians
of that day—that is to say, one-half of the Roundhead party—
had as little tolerance as Laud himself for the like of Bunyan.
They thought that the poor and unlearned were very well,
and that Jack was as good as his master in the eyes of the
Church, but that Jack and his master must both have

their religion provided for them by orthodox Presbyterian ministers. To that idea also Cromwell and his Ironsides said " No." To them " new Presbyter was but old Priest writ large," if the Presbyter tried to interfere with Baptist or Independent congregations, or with the religion of a man's own heart. And it was Cromwell and his men who got the upper hand in the struggle inside the Puritan party. For a dozen eventful years they kept the ring for Puritan religious experiment of all kinds.

But the Puritan rule, though it gave religious freedom to all Puritans, rendered itself intolerable to the Anglicans and to many others besides. England could not find an abiding home under the rule of the Saints, who were more forceful than numerous. So on Cromwell's death it collapsed, and the prison doors of the Restoration closed for a dozen years on John Bunyan.

But, even in the sphere of religion, Cromwell's regime had done work that was never undone. He had given time to the Puritan sects to take root in the island so that no subsequent persecution could eradicate them. And he had secured that the future of English Puritanism outside the Established Church would lie not with an orthodox Presbyterianism of the Scottish model, but in a variety of sects—Bunyan's own Baptists not least among them. Not with orthodox Calvinism, not wholly with Anglicanism in its many forms, did the future of English religion lie. There was a place, and a great place, secured for the spirit of John Bunyan's personal and congregational religion, of which " the foundation is not a doctrinal system but a moral conception."

But there are more things in *Pilgrim's Progress* than the most perfect representation of evangelical religion. You must remember it is not only a great religious tract, but has been hailed as the first English novel. The way of the Pilgrims, and the way of the reader withal, is cheered by the songs, the rural scenery, the tender and humorous human dialogues, which in the Second Part gain ground upon the sterner stuff. Christian seems to have made the way a little smoother or less awful for his wife and children after him. All the delightful machinery of life which accompanies the onward march of the Pilgrims perpetually reminds us what a wonderful place that old England was, now long vanished beyond recall, and almost beyond imagination. In *Pilgrim's Progress* we taste the old rural life with its songs and country mirth, and we hear the sound of the English language already come to perfection and not yet defiled. It is in fact still in great measure the England of Shakespeare, but with Puritanism superadded. Autolycus might accost the Pilgrims on the footpath way and we should feel no surprise. Falstaff might send Bardolph to bid them join him in the wayside tavern.

The language of *Pilgrim's Progress* has two sources—first the Bible, and, secondly and no less, the pure, crisp, telling English then spoken by the common people. From that common source, indeed, the English translators of the Bible had drawn their power of words, alas irrecoverable in our day when a thousand distracting influences have marred common speech and writing in every class of society. " The vocabulary of *Pilgrim's Progress* is the vocabulary of the common people." Indeed, the turns of phrase that were then commonest are often not the least happy. "You have gone a good stitch, you may well be aweary." "A saint abroad and a devil at home." And finally, a remark of Greatheart's to Honest, " By this I know thou art a cock of the right kind "—a phrase savouring of the pastimes of Bunyan's unregenerate days. Macaulay, in his essay on John Bunyan in the *Encyclopædia Britannica*, has thus summed up Bunyan's equipment as an author—" A keen mother wit, a great command of the homely mother tongue, an intimate knowledge of the English Bible, and a vast and dearly-bought spiritual experience."

The country through which the Pilgrims travel, and the road along which they have to pass, is the countryside, the roads and lanes, of the English east Midlands, with which Bunyan was familiar. The sloughs, the robbers, and the other accidents and dangers of the road were real facts of life in the English seventeenth century, the classical period of bad roads, highwaymen and footpads. We must indeed except the dragons and giants; but those too he got from no more alien source than *Sir Bevis of Southampton* and other old English ballads, legends and broadsides that used then to circulate among the common people, instead of the flood of precise newspaper information that kills the imaginative faculty in people to-day. Till his long prison life began, Bunyan, like his fellow-countrymen in general, had dwelt under the same rural influences as the youthful Shakespeare. Men and women were not then buried so deep in the heart of ugly towns that they could know neither beauty nor solitude. Then even the town-dweller had the unspoiled beauty and solitude of nature within ten minutes' walk of his door. This fact goes far to account for the strength and imaginative quality of English religion, language, literature, thought and feeling in those days as compared with our own shallower and more mechanical moods. In those days men were much left alone with nature, with themselves, with God, as they too seldom are under modern conditions of life.

As Blake has said:

" Great things are done when men and mountains meet.
These are not done by scurrying in the street."

This principle is true not only of the mountains that nursed Wordsworth's genius, but also of the far-stretched horizons of the drained fenland and of Cambridgeshire, over which the rising and the sinking sun and the glories of cloud-land were often watched by solitary men—Squire Cromwell for instance, and each of the yeomen farmers who became his Ironsides. In the boundless spaces of the East Anglian countryside each of these men had felt himself to be alone with God, before ever they came together to form a regiment. And that same principle is true of the flats, the lanes and the woodland denes of Bedfordshire, the nurse of Bunyan and of all the strivings and visions of his youth. In his middle age, which he spent in the " den " of his prison, he translated them into *Pilgrim's Progress*.

One quality there is in that book which makes a great part of its charm—the cheerful endurance of suffering and injustice. Such endurance was a great feature of life for Puritan preachers and congregations for a quarter of a century after the Restoration of 1660. Bunyan had his full measure of that experience, long years in prison for preaching, separated from a wife and family whom he loved. He bore it without flinching and without turning sour. Indeed the sweetness of his temper and the happiness of his outlook on life seem to have increased rather than diminished in jail. Doubtless he was calmed and elated by the thought that he was suffering like those of whose yet more terrible sufferings he read so often in the *Book of Martyrs*. That calm and joyous endurance of great wrongs was one of the inspirations of *Pilgrim's Progress*.

There is one fortunate minor circumstance about *Pilgrim's Progress* that has helped to make it one of the most universally accepted books for nearly three centuries past—it has no politics. That negative quality it shares with Shakespeare. Written in prison by a victim of Cavalier vengeance, it can be read with unalloyed pleasure by members of the Anglican communion no less than by inheritors of the Roundhead tradition. Whig and Tory have equally rejoiced in it: a hundred years ago Southey and Macaulay united to press its claims on the notice of the literary world. It is not a party book, nor even in a strict sense a denominational book, but a book which all Englishmen may read, and of which all Englishmen are proud. Bunyan, as some of his less happily conceived writings show, could be a bitter and even scurrilous controversialist on doctrinal subjects. But he kept the spirit of controversy out of *Pilgrim's Progress*, and all through his life he turned a dead, indifferent eye on politics, even when politics put him in prison.

The only recorded political act of his life was its last act, and that was a negative act. He refused the tempting and flattering offers of James II. to enter politics as the supporter of the royal policy of the day—the policy of tolerating and temporarily exalting the Puritan sects at the expense of the Church of England, in order the better to destroy the fundamental laws and the Protestant religion of the land. On that policy John Bunyan, for all that he had suffered from the Church of England, quietly and contemptuously turned his back. Giant Pope, whom he had reported as moribund in the First Part of *Pilgrim's Progress*, had become the formidable " monster " of the Second Part, the dragon with seven heads and ten horns that made great havoc of children. John Bunyan was not the man to be deceived by the flattery of courtiers, or to be made the dupe of the Church of Rome.

A few months later the Revolution of 1688-1689 gave a great measure of liberty and peace to the religious life of the country, endowing the Protestant Free Churches with toleration on a legal and Parliamentary basis. But ere that happy event John Bunyan had been called to cross the Dark River, and never did a braver or a more pure-hearted man obey that summons.

Here, after three hundred years, we meet to celebrate his birth; and the world pays him homage. Seldom has there been such an exaltation of the humble and meek. He shines one of the brightest stars in the firmament of English literature. Yet he had no other ambition in anything he wrote save to turn poor sinners to repentance.

# POOR MUGGLETON AND THE CLASSICS

POOR Muggleton was a failure at the classics. Without the help of Mr Bohn's translations he never could read Greek or any but the simplest Latin, though he had studied little else save those two languages during eight years at school; so he had to be rescued ignominiously by some new-fangled tripos at Cambridge. Hence he writes with the proverbial bitterness of the incompetent on a subject of which he really knows nothing. Only to-day I received from him the following attack on our methods of classical teaching, written in complete ignorance of the reforms that have taken place in it since he was a boy:

" Greek tragedy, unlike Homer and Aristophanes, is the hardest thing in the world of letters to be appreciated by an Englishman with Shakespeare in his blood. The plays require a Verrall to turn them inside out and a Gilbert Murray to translate them into Swinburnian, before I can see something they might have meant—and *didn't* according to some critics! And these masterpieces, requiring the finest subtlety of literary feeling and scholarship in the reader, are selected for the perusal of boys who have not yet mastered Greek grammar and are ignorant of the real values even of English literature. I was actually turned on to read *Hecuba* when I was ten! What was *Hecuba* to me or I to *Hecuba*? I remember feeling vaguely depressed by a mental picture of the poor old lady sitting in the dust at a tent door, but I was not purified by fear and pity. I thought it all strangely dull, whereas Homer and Aristophanes I always understood and felt, even when I had to look out every second word. I dare say the age for beginning Greek tragedy has since been raised to eleven, or even twelve! Who knows? For Reform is afoot in the scholastic world nowadays.

" I am sometimes told that Greek tragedy has to be put

thus early into boys' hands, in order to provide examples of the Iambic verse which they are shortly afterwards required to compose. But why are they asked to compose poetry in a language they have not yet mastered? In the case of any modern language, no schoolmaster would dream of adopting a method so absurd. I only wish I had been taught to read Greek fluently instead of being compelled to translate English into Greek verse. That process was, with my schoolfellows and me, a very remarkable kind of literary occupation. We first looked out all the English words in a dictionary and wrote down the Greek equivalents in their English order; and then we tried to transpose the words thus collected into an order consonant with the rules of Iambic metre, which were to us purely arbitrary and meaningless. It was neither more nor less educative than putting together the pieces of a Chinese puzzle. I have certainly been helped in my understanding of the construction of sentences and the subtlety of language by a rigid course of Latin Prose composition; but Greek composition was quite beyond me, and I believe that only the best scholars have time to learn both properly.

" The fact is," continues Muggleton—[Whenever a man writes " the fact is," or " doubtless," he is always going to rush into the realms of purest fancy or conjecture, as Muggleton now]—" The fact is that the scheme of education now made to serve for the average English upper class boy was devised in its main outlines in the time of Erasmus, in the glorious days *when Learning like a stranger came from far* and lodged in Queens' College, Cambridge. The scheme was then devised, not for many stupid boys, but for a few clever boys; not to prepare them for business, government or general culture, but to enable them to edit ' brown Greek manuscripts,' to ' give us the doctrine of the enclitic *De*,' and rout the Scotists. Almost the sole duty of the learned at that moment in the world's affairs was to master Greek and Latin grammar and edit Greek and Latin texts. And into this ancient mould, contrived for a special purpose long ago fulfilled and done with, the mind of the average little Englishman is still in great measure forced. The thing was already an anachronism and a scandal as long ago as the reign of Charles II., when Eachard, in his famous *Contempt of the Clergy*, pronounced in quite the modern spirit against the methods of classical education common to his day and our own.

" I cannot join in the wish often expressed that a classical education may be preserved for the ordinary boy, because he has never had one yet. But I hope he may get one soon. Hitherto he has always been sacrificed to the real or supposed needs of a scholarly minority. The present system is skilfully contrived to enable a boy of average talents to spend eight years almost exclusively at Latin and Greek, and leave off unable to read at sight either of those languages, save the very simplest Latin."

Poor old Muggleton! This is one of his sore subjects! Yet his bitterness against classical education is not extended to the classics. Hellas herself, the mistress whom he has wooed in vain, he follows with the " old-dog " faithfulness of the rejected lover in comedy. As one who has ceased to hope but not to sigh finds it his chief bliss to watch the lady drive past in the park, so does Muggleton still sit down to his Homer—Greek and English—opening it ever with a secret thrill of reverence. He is often found sitting in front of the Elgin Marbles. And he loves to listen to tales of the spades of Crete. He would never go to Athens in company, or at a season when others were there. But in the summer of 1913 he cunningly designed and executed a feint of visiting the Balkans, ostensibly to see how the Christians in those parts loved one another, but really to emerge thence at Salonika and make a bolt for Athens in the hot season, when no one else would be on the Acropolis! All seems to have gone well, for I received the following from him, written at Salonika:

" No, I don't care whether the Bulgarian troops round

the corner have their throats cut, or cut the throats of the Greeks, though clearly one or the other will happen before the month is out. I am sitting on the balcony, looking over the busy little modern port at a better world and a greater epoch in Levantine history, looking at Olympus across the shining waters of the Ægean, across the bay where Xerxes' fleet rode at anchor when it had come through the canal of Athos; I am on the spot—it may be—where he sat to review it. His army must have been camped in the great plain behind, across which our slow train dragged us yesterday from Monastir. It was as he approached Therma (=Salonika) that the lions attacked his camels. And then, says Herodotus, *Xerxes seeing from Therma the mountains of Thessaly, Olympus* . . . Well, there across the bay is Olympus, *seen from Therma* still, though no longer by Xerxes, crowned with snow in June, girdled with rocks, cleft with gullies and wrapped round its base with white morning clouds, which leave it above, alone in æther, in a world far from ours. So it stood for æons before the first fair-haired Achæan warriors came across the plain from the north, seeking sunnier lands by this gay blue sea. So it stood when they looked at it and wondered what lands lay beyond, hidden by it, and went south to see, and stayed, for the lands were good and they and their children might dwell there. So it stood, when Xerxes looked at it from here, and his courtiers, it may be, told him that the Hellenes deemed that their gods dwelt on the summit. By the issue of that happier *Turkish war* of old, when first 'the barbarian' came, it was decided whether that mountain should be as other mountains which have been clothed with legends by the valley-dwellers and seafarers at their base—legends that rested on them awhile and melted off like the summer snow and were forgotten; or whether after some 2500 years the bare sight of that mountain and the knowledge of its name should be to a traveller from an island beyond the limits of the world the one sight that he could not endure to see without tears, though he had passed through lands just liberated and villages desolated by war—because no place on earth could win of him such reverence, were it not that there is a city beyond that mountain."

From a subsequent letter I gather that the city referred to is Athens. Muggleton was not seasick on the voyage from Salonika to Chalcis, so he was able to imagine himself on board an Athenian trireme at Artemisium, beating up and down the straits of Eubœa in alternate fits of pluck and panic during Thermopylæ week. Luckily it was midnight when he went by Thermopylæ, so he missed the disillusionment of seeing the famous pass now broadened by the retirement of the sea. He saw it all, vaguely, by a Byronic moon, weaving " her bright chain o'er the deep," and could imagine that the lights at the foot of the mountains were the torches of the barbarians preparing to attack Leonidas at dawn.

So next week I got this letter from Muggleton, dated 7 A.M., from " the roof of the Parthenon":

" You are still in bed. I am on the high top gallant of the world. The Acropolis opens at dawn and I have had an hour here *alone*! There was one guardian on the scene with whom I made friends over a little wild bird he had caught and was nursing. He let me into the staircase that leads on to the roof of the Parthenon and locked me in. I say 'roof,' though roof there is none, but I am sitting on the top of the unroofed marble walls. A few inches under my left foot is the riders' frieze—for Elgin left the west side of it. I crossed on to the top of the outer or pediment wall and thence looked back and saw the frieze at close quarters, hailing the youth in the felt hat whom I have long loved in casts and photographs. There he still rides, as Phidias taught him, with head half bent; only the back rim of his hat is broken off into mere outline by Time. Then I crossed by a breach in the marble cliffs on to the pediment—the ledge where the Elgin Marbles used to sit—and made my way along it, like a mortal on Olympus while the gods are away. At the other end of the pediment are the two

63

remaining statues, male and female, in an awful and religious solitude. There these two now sit alone, 'strength and beauty met together,' looking over Ægina and Salamis, and waiting for the end of the world. Now I have stood beside them; I have made my pilgrimage and touched the gods of my idolatry.

"No description can give you Athens. If you feel that these were the greatest people in the world, who invented freedom, art, literature and thought, and if, so feeling, you stand on the Acropolis and see all the undoubted places in which they did it, with the old school-familiar names upon them—Pnyx, Parthenon, Dionysus' Theatre, Salamis Bay —all blent together in a harmony of reds and greys, yellows and olive-greens, with purple hills beyond to crown Cephisus' vale as yesterday at sunset—why then, not Rome has anything like it to show the heart.

"A stone's-throw from the Parthenon stands the Erechtheum, loveliest of buildings in the Ionic style as the Parthenon is the grandest in the Doric. Fifty years only parts them, the second great fifty years of Athenian history, yet the change from one perfect form of architecture and ornament to another was made as easily as when a sleeper turns on his side.

"The modern town has kindly built itself far away not merely from the summit of the Acropolis but from the site of the greatest places below. There, for instance, is the Areopagus, a *kopje* or *limestone outcrop*, as naked and as primæval to-day as it was when Orestes and other less mythical personages were tried there. The cave underneath was where the Furies lived. The modern town, where it is permitted to appear, is most inoffensive and does duty in the spectacle for the old one, its tiles forming part of the colour scheme in the view from up here. Nothing in the landscape distracts the eye in its leap from the Acropolis to the hills and islands on the horizon—corresponding to Alban and Sabine hills in the Janiculan view. Ægina, in the middle distance, is really as far away from here as Dover from Calais, but in this clear atmosphere the *distance* only begins with Argolis beyond.

" It is half-past eight, and already as I sit up here the sun is reverberating off Pericles' huge marble blocks. The birds are going in and out of the holes in the smooth, white walls. Not that the walls are ruinous, for what is left of the Parthenon is most beautifully cared for and repaired. New marble blocks, carefully dated 1872, 1902, 1911, as the case may be, are put in where required to hold it together.

" What irony that this, the central hall of the civilized world, should have stood complete during the 1200 years when mankind was too barbarous to care about it, and was blown up by Christians and Moslems between them in 1678, just before the West returned to worship it. Think of those thousand years, when the sun rose and set every day on the Parthenon standing in perfect beauty, uncared for by the savage tribes of men. Even the ruins are worth to us any other ten buildings. For here the plant ' man ' first shot up aloft into æther. From primal brushwood suddenly he grew up straight into an oak of which the head touched heaven; and in the branches such birds sang and such fruits hung as never since are seen or heard. Since then we have all been smaller offshoots of that tree, save when the brushwood reconquers territory, as it often does and has most sadly here, with its squat Turkish fungus, followed by the merry little scrub-oak Greek of to-day, to whom I wish all good things. But here, where for once the holy spirit of man . . ."

Here Muggleton grows speculative; enough, enough!

# POETRY AND REBELLION[1]

WHEN a foreign author, counted among the most distinguished critics in Europe, has written a book on a great period of our national poetry, it is certain to contain some views not altogether English, and therefore all the more instructive for Englishmen. We have previously heard George Brandes on Shakespeare; we have now the opportunity, thanks to this translation of a work which appeared thirty years ago in the original Danish, to hear him on that other poetical constellation which has no central sun, but which, in its total force of light and heat, perhaps rivals the Elizabethan—on Wordsworth, Coleridge, Scott, Keats, Shelley, Byron, and those lesser planets (the foils to their brightness), Southey, Moore, Campbell, Landor. In these Mr Brandes finds his theme; but the fiery comet Blake apparently never swam into his ken.

If we had to give up either these or the Elizabethans, there are some reasons, not indeed sufficient, why we should prefer to part with Shakespeare. They are six giants against one colossus. And although the body of Shakespeare's work is left, he himself is but dimly known to us, while the lives of the moderns are as familiar as their poems. They were fortunate in their friends, at least they were posthumously fortunate in their friends' biographical powers; the records of Hogg, Trelawny, De Quincey, Lamb, Leigh Hunt and Lockhart—and Keats' and Byron's own letters—show to what height of beauty and power, if also at times of folly, it has been possible for the human spirit to attain. But no one looks to find such matter in the gleanings which Mr Sidney Lee has so scrupulously gathered behind the harvest that time has carried away. Further, we suspect that even if

[1] *Main Currents in Nineteenth Century Literature*: IV. *Naturalism in England.* George Brandes. (Heinemann, 1905.) (Translated from Danish of 1875.) This essay is revised from an article which appeared in the *Independent Review* in 1905.

we knew him, Shakespeare, unlike his poetry, would prove too perfect, too wise, and too bourgeois in the best sense to have the picturesque charm of the Inspired Charity Boy, the Ineffectual Angel, or the Pilgrim of Eternity. But this we shall never know. For, however many thousands of years our civilization may last, neither we nor our remotest descendants will ever see into the Mermaid Tavern. Its doors are closed, its windows shuttered, Time Past has got the key, and our scholars can only sweep the doorstep.

Then, too, Shakespeare did not take part in the Gunpowder Plot, or write satires on James and Cecil, or sail with the Sea Beggars, or die defending Rochelle. But the moderns, whether or not they prove to be " for all time," were at least no small part of their own stirring age. The times were great and the literary gentlemen were not small. Their alchemy has resolved each of the dark, hot and heavy political passions of their own day into its corresponding poetical essence. They are the Radicals and the Tories of Eternity. They founded Pantisocratic Societies and Quarterly Reviews. They were stalked over the Quantock Hills by Pitt's spies, as they plotted the downfall of Pope beside " the ribbed sea sand." They sang of Highland clansmen and of knights in armour, and poetic Toryism sprang on to the stage, fully bedizened, out of Sir Walter's head. Others of them defied the gods of the Holy Alliance, concentrated on their own heads the whole weight of tyranny's anathema, and rode down the Pisan Lungarno in the face of Austria, England and Italy :

" Dowered with the hate of hate, the scorn of scorn,
　　　　The love of love."

Four things, rarely united, combine to enhance their story: great poetic genius; great personal eccentricity and power; great principles come to issue in politics; and the picturesque surroundings of the old world in its last generation of untarnished beauty. Except Tolstoi, with his smock and his weather-beaten face, standing among the Russian snows and revolutions, there has been no figure in our own

POETRY AND REBELLION

time that exerted the same sway over the imagination of
Europe. Even in the Victorian era our great poets paid
their debt to society by inspecting Board Schools instead of
joining rebellions in Hellas and in Italy. For centuries to
come, the eyes of men somewhat weary with the dull drab
of their own generations will be turned to the funeral pyre
of Shelley on the shore of the blue Mediterranean, with the
marble mountains of Carrara behind, "touching the air
with coolness," the heart of hearts unconsumed in the flame
and the doomed figure beside it looking out to sea. The
prayer of old Europe for liberty and new life seems to rise
up to the skies in that sacrificial flame "waving and quiver-
ing with a brightness of inconceivable beauty." Such is
the romance that England once gave mankind, to show
what poetry she can create when her heart is turned for a
moment from the cares of the world to the things of the
imagination and the mind.

It is these outward suits and trappings of poetry—its
historical, political and personal accidents—of which Mr
Brandes' book gives a brilliant survey. Not a paragraph is
unmeaning or trite. His method of treating the poetry itself
is to analyse these external accompaniments. He scarcely
attempts to judge the style, but only the content; he does
not place the writers in order of their merit as poets, but in
order of their effectiveness as revolutionaries. For instance,
Wordsworth is introduced as the tyrannicide who slew Pope,
and led the exodus of the English poets back to nature;
but he is cast aside when he invests himself in the "strait-
jacket of orthodox piety." That is Mr Brandes' account of
the matter, where most people are content to say that
Wordsworth first wrote good poetry and then bad:

"Two voices are there: one is of the deep,

And one is of an old half-witted sheep;

And, Wordsworth, both are thine."

68

# POETRY AND REBELLION

Mr Brandes makes it his task to appraise each poet in turn, according as he adds some new element to the rebellious growth of literary, religious or political "naturalism." Wordsworth begins the return to nature; Coleridge adds "naturalistic romanticism"; Scott, "historical naturalism"; Keats, "all-embracing sensuousness"; Landor, "republican humanism"; Shelley, "radical naturalism"; but Byron is the "culmination of naturalism," and has seven whole chapters to himself, while none of the commoners has more than two. Each new element is analysed, each character and personality described with an insight that never fails and a sympathy that fails only in the case of Wordsworth.

Now this method, which really consists in talking all round the subject of poetry but never plucking out its heart, is the best as a means of stimulating the love of poetry in the young and of introducing readers to a particular group of poets. It is interesting, picturesque, alive. It gives the colour, the setting, the intellectual formulas that contained the poetic essence. But that essence it does not attempt to define.

By thus limiting the range of his inquiry, Mr Brandes has saved himself from disaster, for we are left with the impression that if he had told us which were the best poems, we should have been asked to regard *Cain* and *Don Juan* as the "culmination" not only of "naturalism," but of English poetry. Incidentally he lets it slip out that Burns was a "much more gifted poet" than Wordsworth. But these views are of no consequence, because not obtruded. The brilliant and suggestive analysis of the content, fortified by long and well-chosen quotations, enables the reader to form his own judgment on the style. Now one's own judgment on poetry is the only judgment worth having, not because it is necessarily right, but because it alone is strongly felt. The value of the appreciation of poetry lies, not in mere correctness of opinion, but in combined rightness and depth of feeling. Therefore the critic, even if he were infallible, would do well to leave the final judgment to the reader.

For these reasons, I believe that this introduction is the best existing introduction to the poets and poetry of this period as a whole. The errors of the book are not such as could possibly deceive our present literary public, while its truth would add something new to their stock of ideas. It is only if people understand what the system of political and religious persecution was like when these poets were young that they can do justice to the merits, while they detect the errors, of Mr Brandes' book. What was it (other than the law of marriage) against which Shelley and Byron, as formerly Wordsworth and Coleridge, declared themselves rebels? What justification has Mr Brandes for such language as this?—

"The *neutral* qualities of the nation were educated into bad ones. Self-esteem and firmness were nursed into that hard-heartedness of the aristocratic and that selfishness of the commercial classes which always distinguish a period of reaction; loyalty was excited into servility, and patriotism into the hatred of other nations. And the national *bad* qualities were over-developed. The desire for outward decorum at any price, which is the shady side of the moral impulse, was developed into hypocrisy in the domain of morality; and that determined adherence to the established religion, which is the least attractive outcome of a practical and not profoundly reasoning turn of mind, was fanned either into hypocrisy or active intolerance."

This is the picture, the "political background," which Mr Brandes has sketched for his panorama. Is it over-charged? I think not; but to show this I must call attention to a few facts not generally emphasized in our historical text-books. And before doing this I will quote another passage, which clearly shows that Mr Brandes is not pre-judiced against England. He sees the faults of Englishmen, but he admires the Englishman.

"Beneath that attachment to the soil, and that delight in encountering and mastering the fitful humours of the sea, which are the deep-seated causes of Naturalism, there is in the Englishman the still deeper-seated national feelings which, under the peculiar historical conditions of this period, naturally led the cleverest men of the day in the direction of Radicalism. No nation is so thoroughly penetrated by the feeling of personal independence as England.

" It took an Englishman to do what Byron did, stem alone the stream which flowed from the fountain of the Holy Alliance. . . . But an Englishman, too, was needed to fling the gauntlet boldly and defiantly in the face of his own people."

And Mr Brandes appreciates no less warmly the character of the Tory Scott—all in him that was " racy of the soil " of North Britain.

In the generation following 1792 Britain was not a free country. The island was governed by a certain number of privileged persons, and the bulk of the inhabitants not only had no share of any sort in the government, but they were debarred from demanding a share by laws specially enacted for this purpose and savagely administered. In politics and religion, a system like Strafford's " thorough " ruled the land under the forms of Statute and Common Law.

This revived Straffordism had two periods of activity: one in the last decade of the eighteenth century, in the radical days of Coleridge and Wordsworth; the other after Waterloo, in the time of Shelley and Byron. In the intervening years, 1800 to 1815, British liberty, gagged by Pitt's previous legislation, gave no sign of life; and indeed everyone was preoccupied with the pressing danger of conquest by Napoleon. After Waterloo came the second period of conflict; but then the Tory ministers were only acting on the principles and re-enforcing the measures of twenty years before. It is, therefore, to the earlier period that we must look for the heroic age of tyranny, when Burke, finding in the French Revolution a subject as great as his own genius, first inspired our statesmen with the un-English desire to prevent all further development of religious and political thought, and to root out the spirit of independence.

An agitation for Parliamentary Reform, begun by the middle classes of Yorkshire in the eighties, had spread, under the influence of the French Revolution, to some of the lower classes in London; these men began, in 1793 and 1794, to hold orderly public meetings in the suburbs, where speeches were delivered in favour of Parliamentary Reform and of the new principle of Democracy. Thereupon Acts were passed enabling a single magistrate to disperse a meeting at will, and making death the penalty for disobedience to his orders. The result was that no one attempted to hold such meetings again till after Waterloo. The upper classes were mad, inevitably and in part excusably mad, with fear of the French Revolution. In their blind panic they saw Englishmen as Jacobins walking.

They so little knew their countrymen, and so little understood the causes of what was going on in France, that they feared a repetition of the same phenomena in this island, where there was neither the fuel nor the fire for such a conflagration. Pitt put a stop even to lectures given by his opponents, and soon afterwards political associations and trade unions were universally suppressed by law. All Liberal politicians, except the few who held seats in Parliament, were driven back into private life, and even there they were followed by Government spies—sinister figures unfamiliar to the freeborn Englishman, but evoked by the passions of that unhappy time. Meanwhile the Press was effectually gagged, for the juries readily sent publishers to prison, at the dictation of the law officers of the Crown. The demand for Parliamentary Reform was punished in Scotland by transportation, in England by imprisonment for sedition; under this treatment it ceased to make itself heard before the century of enlightenment closed in darkness and in fear.[1]

---

[1] So abject was the terrorism produced by the prosecutions that in 1795 even honest old Major Cartwright, " the father of constitutional reformers," could not get any publisher to take his work in favour of Parliamentary

# POETRY AND REBELLION

Such was the system which Fox denounced as destructive to " the spirit, the fire, the freedom, the boldness, the energy of the British character, and with them its best virtue." The man who used this language was more truly a Briton than the ministers who sent spies to betray the private conversation of their countrymen, and taught the English for a while to abase their spirit like the tame nations who fawned on Napoleon and Metternich. Fox " a Briton died," but he also lived a Briton: his traducers, who then and since have assumed to themselves all the " patriotic " virtues, did not seem to understand that to be a Briton means to speak your mind without fear.

The measures of coercion, as Mr Brandes points out, killed independence of character and made an end of the free play of intellect and imagination. The revival, twenty years later, could only be effected by violent, and not altogether wholesome, literary stimulants. And if Byron attacked morality as well as despotism, he had at least been provoked to this unfortunate conflict by the hypocrisy which had long pretended, for party purposes, that morals were the peculiar preserve of orthodoxy and Toryism. The whole movement of coercion had been a religious movement, as can be seen in the Government writers from Burke and the Anti-Jacobin downwards. There was much that was noble in the evangelicalism that defied Napoleon and afterwards freed the slave. But closely connected with this, and often indistinguishable from it, was religion in its most odious form, not a moral influence, but an influence pretending to a monopoly in morals; not a martyr defying the strong, but an inquisitor punishing the weak. An attempt was made, with considerable success, to eradicate the very

Reform, but had to " hire a shop and servant " to sell it. See *Mock and Constitutional Reform* (1810), p. 47.
[NOTE, 1929; I leave these paragraphs as I wrote them a quarter of a century ago. They are true, if not the whole truth. Now, after the experience of 1914-1918, I have come to regard the suppression of English liberties as an " inevitable " consequence of the war with revolutionary France. But the " inevitable," especially in war-time, is often very evil.]

slight traces of free thought then observable in England and to reduce by persecution the power even of orthodox dissent. A few examples will serve to illustrate the spirit of the system.

Paine's *Age of Reason*—an argument grounding religion on Deism and the belief in Immortality—was directed equally against the Atheism then prevalent in France and the Biblical literalism then universal in England; it was highly moral and earnest in its tone, but sometimes violent in its language against the ethics of the Old Testament and the miraculous elements in the New. In 1797 an English publisher of this work, Williams by name, was prosecuted by the Society for the Suppression of Vice and Immorality. Williams was himself a Christian; he had a large family; he was abjectly poor; he repented, and he begged, after the case had gone against him, that Wilberforce and his Committee of Bishops would not bring him up for judgment. This prayer was urged on humanitarian grounds by Erskine, on this occasion counsel for the prosecution, who had found his victim stitching tracts in a wretched little room, where his children were suffering with smallpox. But the godly men were " firm," as Wilberforce boasts in his diary, and proceeded to ruin the miserable family in the name of Christ. If this was the spirit of Wilberforce, when impelled by fanaticism, we can imagine what was the spirit of less humane men. Twenty years later, times had not changed; for in the year of Peterloo, Richard Carlile, his wife and shop assistants, were imprisoned for republishing Paine's *Age of Reason*.

Meanwhile the campaign of slander was carried on in the alleged interests of morality. One instance will suffice, from the very highest type of Tory literature—the *Beauties of the Anti-Jacobin* (1799). In a note on Canning's wittiest poem, *The New Morality*, we read that Coleridge " has now quitted the country, become a citizen of the world, left his little ones fatherless, and his wife destitute. *Ex uno disce* his associates Southey and Lambe " (*sic*). Here are Anti-Jacobin accuracy and logic in a nutshell. In the cause of religion and morality a lie is told—that Coleridge in 1799 had deserted his wife and children. In the next sentence the deduction is made. It is stated that Southey and Lamb, because they associate with a Unitarian and Radical like Coleridge, may be pilloried as the sort of people who desert their wives and children. Society is duly warned against a scoundrel like Charles Lamb! He is the sort of person who breaks up family life!

Priestley was a scientist of European reputation, and a Unitarian of the Biblical school, an avowed opponent of Paine and the Deists. He was driven from the country by the social persecution roused against him by the clergy and the " Church and King " mob, who could not suffer a Socinian to live in England. And if Priestley had to retire to America, we can imagine how unendurable life was made to his humbler followers. Nor were orthodox dissenters under cover. Not only did Nonconformists remain excluded from the universities and from numerous civil rights, but a social persecution was now directed against them; some were forced to abandon their business in the towns and to fly to America, while the position of dissenters on the estates of Tory landowners was often rendered untenable. To this persecution it was the design of the Cabinet in the year 1800 to give legislative force. The design to go back on the Toleration Act of 1688 so far got a hold of Pitt's mind that he was diverted from his purpose only by the appeals of Wilberforce. The hypocrites and formalists were stopped from further progress on the path of persecution by the man of real religion. For Wilberforce, while he pursued Deism with the sharpest edge of the law, while he stirred up the educated classes to regard Priestley's views with a horror of which their Laodicean ancestors had been innocent, knew that the Gospel had true though erring friends in the orthodox Nonconformists. He therefore checked the design, which would, as he said, at once have filled the jails with the best of the dissenting ministers. But that the Cabinet should have seriously considered such iniquity shows what was the spirit of the age.

75

The legal persecution of nonconformity had been suggested to Pitt by Bishop Pretyman [1]—the type of the clergyman of that day, hostile to every earnest movement within the Church, whether evangelical or other, but stringent to put down the unorthodox and the dissenters by law, and shameless in the pursuit of the loaves and fishes. He finally made use of his position as Pitt's old tutor and friend to ask his pupil to make him Archbishop of Canterbury [2]; the best use of the prerogative ever made by George III. was to veto this scandalous job. In Ireland the bishops added open vice to the characteristics of their English brethren. " In the north," wrote the Primate of Ireland in 1801, " I have six bishops under me. Three are men of tolerable moral character, but are inactive and useless, and two are of acknowledged bad character. Fix Mr Beresford at Kilmore, and we shall then have three very inactive bishops, and, what I trust the world has not yet seen, three bishops in one district reported to be the most profligate men in Europe." [3] At Kilmore Mr Beresford was duly fixed.

Such was the Church which in the name of morality urged the State to suppress every movement of thought. For the cry had been raised which used most easily to appeal to the English ear, that the foundations of morality were in danger. In the eighteenth century the governing class had been openly profligate, and some of George III.'s favourite ministers had been among the worst. That caused no alarm. But when democracy showed its head the Tories became the patrons, though not always the examples, of morality. The silly marriage theory promulgated by the philosopher Godwin gave his enemies their cue. Family life was being undermined by the Jacobins! If the standard of English morals was not high the Continental standard was lower still, and it was easy, therefore, for our alarmists to call attention to the Continental standard, and to ascribe

[1] *Life of Wilberforce*, ii., pp. 360-365.
[2] *Rose's Diaries*, ii., pp. 82-89.
[3] MacDonagh, *The Viceroy's Post-Bag*, p. 99.

to the teaching of Jacobinism evils that had been rampant in the days of Louis XIV. Canning's satires are full of this idea; and one of the most distinguished men of learning in the United Kingdom solemnly wrote a book to prove that Frederick William II. of Prussia was the saviour of social morality, because he had suppressed free thought in his dominions by force—Frederick William, religious mystic and voluptuary, who even in his debauches never forgot to be pious, and who caused the Lutheran clergy solemnly to legalize and sanctify his bigamy![1] With Frederick William thus recognized by the Tories as a saviour of society, we can understand why Byron afterwards plunged to the assault of throne, altar and hearth together.

Hypocrisy was the order of the day. The word "freedom" was, by a masterpiece of irony, retained in the official cant. When Pitt introduced his Seditious Meetings Bill into the House he spoke large words on the undoubted right of the people to that freedom of speech of which the measure was designed to deprive them. " The perfect freedom, civil and religious, which we enjoy in this happy country" became the cant phrase of the persecutors. Even Scottish writers, the countrymen of Muir and Palmer, in books written to argue that religious persecution is a duty of the State, could talk of our Constitution as one in which each man sits " under his own vine, and under his own fig-tree, and there is none to make him afraid."[2] Language like this has to a large extent imposed upon posterity, but it goaded contemporaries like Byron to madness.

Another form of hypocrisy was to inveigh perpetually against the cruelties exercised by the French revolutionists as being the peculiar results of liberal principles, while our allies, the despots, were perpetrating like acts in Poland without even a shadow of excuse, and threatening them against France in Brunswick manifestos; and while we

---

[1] *Proofs of Conspiracy*, Robinson, 1797 (dedicated to Secretary Windham), pp. 90-92, 276, 283, 316-317.   For the private life and public policy of Frederick William II. see Sorel, *L'Europe et la Rév. Fr.*, i. 478-496.

[2] *Proofs of Conspiracy*, pp. 94, 446.

ourselves were torturing the Irish by flogging and pitch-capping as a regular system. The torture was condoned over here, just as the Terror was condoned in France, as being the only means of self-preservation in time of deadly peril. Whether massacre without torture, or torture reduced to a system, be the worse, it is for casuists to decide. But whereas Robespierre and Carrier of Nantes paid the penalty of their crimes at the hands of their fellow-revolutionists as soon as the worst danger of civil war and invasion had passed, Judkin Fitzgerald was shielded by special Act of Parliament from the natural legal consequence of his crimes, and was raised to the Honourable Order of Baronets. That men who condoned and rewarded Fitzgerald should accuse the Jacobins of inhumanity is the kind of thing that astounds those who have not been brought up in the English tradition. And it has not escaped Mr Brandes.[1]

This system of hypocrisy and tyranny, in the course of its long struggle with the yet more tyrannical though possibly more useful revolutionary governments of France, success-fully smothered the first stirrings of radical and free thought. The appalling failure of the French Revolution to establish liberty turned over Coleridge, Wordsworth, Southey and many others to join the reaction here. Fox died. Then came Waterloo and the restoration of the *ancien régime* throughout the European world. Thereupon Radicalism in England again attempted to lift its head, stung by the economic miseries of the mass of the people, but was stamped down once more by repressive measures associated in the minds of the victims with the name of Castlereagh, who intro-duced the " Six Acts " into the House of Commons. That was the era when Byron's poetry suddenly became a force in politics.

I have set down these few facts to explain what Mr Brandes calls " the political background " of his book, and

[1] Brandes, pp. 154-155. Lecky, *History of England*, 1890 ed., viii., pp. 22-30. *State Trials*, xxvii., pp. 759-820

to justify the high importance and value which he attaches
to Byron's place in history.  The true splendour of Byron
lay in his instinct to rebellion, in which the pride of the
aristocrat and the self-assertion of the egoist against the
society that rebukes him were compounded with a generous
rage for public justice and a democratic sympathy with the
poor.  His service to mankind was this, that in the hour
of universal repression and discouragement he made all
England and all Europe hear the note of everlasting de-
fiance.  He was called satanic: there have been moments
in history when the qualities of Milton's Satan are needed
to save mankind:

> " Yet, Freedom! yet thy banner, torn, but flying,
>   Streams like the thunderstorm *against* the wind."

He spoke, and the oppressor looked pitiable, and the inquisitor stood naked to the scorn of the world; the laugh at last
was turned against the Anti-Jacobin.  The Government no
more dared silence him than the Russian Government dared
silence Tolstoi.  His previous literary fame, his personal
prestige, the very force of the offending satires, made it
impossible to institute proceedings against the *Dedication of
Don Juan, The Age of Bronze*, or the *Vision of Judgment*.
But although the first crash of Byron's thunder could
scarcely have been louder or more electric, the destructive
bolts might have been more wisely aimed.  He might then
have exerted a more lasting influence upon England, where
even liberals soon said that the " thunder's roll " had
" taught them little." [1]  And though abroad the Byronic
cult has had length of days that are not yet at an end, it
might well have been the religion of a purer humanity.  Mr
Brandes sees this, but he will not call attention to the spots
on his sun.

[1] I am not raising the question whether Matthew Arnold is to be counted
as a " liberal " or not.  It is characteristic of him that he has packed into
two sonnets," To a Republican Friend, 1848," the higher faith of Liberalism
and the higher wisdom of Conservatism in lines so admirable that every
good citizen ought to know them by heart.

# POETRY AND REBELLION

I have already indicated, in describing the claim set up by the reactionaries to be considered as the high priests of virtue, how the atmosphere of the time provoked Byron to confound the hearth with the altar and the throne. The temptation no doubt was strong, but he could have resisted it if there had not been a weak place in his own armour. His cynical view of private morals, so different from the generosity of his political passions, was connected with his old-fashioned and essentially aristocratic ideas of women. This deficiency in his equipment as a rebel has escaped Mr Brandes' attention. Byron was not revolutionary enough : his ideas of male supremacy were those of the *ancien régime*. He understood the rights of man, but he seems never to have heard of the rights of woman. Yet the idea had already been set afloat among our English radicals, though only in the crudest form. Shorn of its coarseness and hardness, Mary Wollstonecraft's *Rights of Women* was in her day a great advance in social thought. It is a vulgar error to suppose that the book contains a single word against marriage; but it claims education for women, on the ground that the relation of the sexes must be essentially intellectual and moral, not sensual and trivial. All such ideas were to the creator of Juan and Haidee no less ridiculous than to Lord Eldon or George III. " You must have observed," says Byron, " that I give my heroines extreme refinement, joined to great simplicity and want of education ": this cheap surrender to the " manly " ideal of " the fair sex " largely accounts for the popularity of his works with the vulgar and the conventional. The moment he touched on women Byron was the dandy and grand seigneur. He thus writes (8th November 1819) of the Countess Guiccioli: " As neither her birth, nor her rank, nor connections of birth or marriage are inferior to my own, I am in honour bound to support her through." What revolutionary sentiments! What justice and equality is here implied to the Guiccioli's humbler sisters! The truth is that the deliverer of Greece had not " doubled Cape Turk." Mr Brandes might have pointed out this fact in one of his seven chapters on Byron, without sinning against the rigidity of his own liberalism.

Again, Mr Brandes treats the Byronic philosophy of life with the same respect with which he treats the Byronic politics. This seems a mistake. So, too, some of the pages devoted to the content of Byron's nature poetry might have been better spent on Wordsworth's. Is *Manfred* really "matchless as an Alpine landscape"? It has some formidable rivals! The true poetry of nature, and of the then newly discovered Alps, may rather be sought in Coleridge's *Hymn to Mont Blanc*, in Shelley's *Prometheus* (Act ii., sc. 3), and above all in the Sixth Book of Wordsworth's *Prelude*, with all the absurd, pleasing, trivial realism of the walking tour, lighted by occasional gleams of solemn grandeur wherein the mountains are revealed as the symbol of something too great for our comprehension.

Mr Brandes in no way underestimates the value of the content of Shelley's poetry. He says, speaking of the birth at Field Place in August 1792, that his "life was to be of greater and more enduring significance in the emancipation of the human mind than all that happened in France" even in that great month. Here, surely, he is more in the right than Matthew Arnold. Because Shelley does not, like Byron, deal with politics and daily life, he is not therefore "ineffectual." It is through his poetry that we occasionally get glimpses into that other sphere of passions not of this earth:

> "Nor seeks nor finds he mortal blisses,
> But feeds on the aerial kisses
> Of shapes that haunt thought's wildernesses."

It is indeed true that, whenever Shelley tried to apply the standards of his world to the hard facts of ours, he made himself, at best, ridiculous. As an influence on politics in his own day he was nothing. His cry after "something afar from the sphere of our sorrow" died away like faint music

F        81

over the heads of the men whom Byron summoned to the barricades:

> " Ad arma, cessantes ad arma
> Concitet, imperiumque frangat."

But now that Metternich and Castlereagh are no more, and Garibaldi's statue is safe on the Janiculum, and the ages still go by bringing to Western Europe subtler oppressions and larger liberties; now that we must apply our minds to " Riddles of death Thebes never knew "—now it is that we find best of all in Shelley's poetry the atmosphere which can truly be called Freedom, the zeal for the unfettered pursuit of truth and of justice and of beauty; in each fresh generation, youth will for ever be setting out on some new voyage for which the last chorus in *Hellas* is the sailors' chant of departure. This idea Mr Brandes has well expressed as follows:

" When Shelley sings to liberty, we feel that this liberty is not a thing which we can grasp with our hands, or confer as a gift in a constitution, or inscribe among the articles of a state church," or, one might surely add, on the programme of a revolutionary club! " It is the eternal cry of the human spirit, its never-ending requirement of itself; it is the spark of heavenly fire which Prometheus placed in the human heart when he formed it, and which it has been the work of the greatest among men to fan into the flame that is the source of all light and all warmth in those who feel that life would be dark as the grave and cold as stone without it."

But liberty, even Shelley's liberty, is not an end but a means. This brings us at last to issue with the central idea of Mr Brandes' book. Liberty, indeed, is the indispensable condition of any noble function of the soul—a condition so seldom realized, to be won in the first instance only by such determined and painful warfare, and retained only by so constant a watch upon our conduct and its motives, that it is no wonder if those few who know the value and the rarity of freedom sometimes make the error of supposing it to be the end of life. Yet it is not the end but the means. The mischief is that the majority of men who do not regard it as an end greatly underestimate its importance as a means, or think that they have got it when they are only following some conventional standard.

And as with life, so with poetry, which is the essence of life. The condition of poetry is freedom, but the content of poetry is joy, sorrow, beauty, love, man's awe at the strength and his hope in the beneficence of those unknown powers upon whose lap all living things are cradled. Poetry must speak not merely, or even chiefly, as Mr Brandes seems to think, of liberty, but of all that the human spirit desires and fears. It is because Shelley has created his goddess Liberty in the image of all these things that she has some reality as an object for our devotion; there is little to distinguish his liberty from those spiritual and material forces of nature to which he appeals in the *Ode to the West Wind*. And all the great passions of the heart and of the intellect find expression in Wordsworth, Coleridge, Shelley and Keats. Mr Brandes comprehends all these passions, but his heart is stirred most deeply by the note of rebellion. Hence, after doing full justice to Coleridge, Scott, Keats and Shelley, he dwells longer and more lovingly on Byron. " In the First Canto of *Childe Harold*," he says, " we already find the *love of freedom* exalted as the one force capable of emancipating from the despair with which the universal misery (the *Weltschmerz*, as the Germans call it) has overwhelmed the soul." The prescription is too limited to cope with a disease so general. It is only for particular individuals in special epochs of history that the love of liberty by itself alone can be enough to ennoble life. Byron in the age of Metternich was perhaps a case in point, but Byron was neither an ordinary person nor ordinarily situated—nor altogether satisfactory. And, after all, the reason why it was good to overthrow Metternich was that we might advance freely to the positive values of life which Byron so often affected to deny.

# POETRY AND REBELLION

Liberty, then, is not the last, but the first, word in human affairs. Its spirit must envelop and preserve the poet, lest he suffer decay, like Wordsworth and Tennyson growing thistle-headed in old age. But his eye must be fixed on things of more positive value. In an age of tyranny and hypocrisy, such as I have described, this atmosphere of liberty had perforce to materialize into rebellion, as in Coleridge and Wordsworth in their youth, and in Shelley and Byron. Keats, indeed, with that wonderful artist's sanity of his, remained an onlooker with strong liberal sympathies, rather than an active rebel. He never belonged to a "Pantisocratic" society. And it was easy for Browning and Meredith to find "liberty" enough in this attitude, in an age of comparative freedom. But by whatever means, whether by rebellion or otherwise, each kept the windows of his mind clear, the chief value of their work (except only in Byron's case) lay not in the wars they waged, but in the things for which alone it is worth while to wage war.

Blessed be the Quantock Hills, blazing with bell-heather above Somerset's green lanes and sea; and blessed among English summers be that of 1797! For there and then did Coleridge and Wordsworth, no less creative than young Buonaparte in the Italian fields, plan out the downfall of Pope and of the *ancien régime* in letters. If the spy whom Pitt sent to watch them had fathomed their real design, and its ultimate effect on the established order of things literary and spiritual, what a report the honest fellow might have sent his master! Perhaps in the style of Carlyle's *Cagliostro's Prophecy*: "Ha! What see I? All the Alexandrines in creation are burnt up! . . ."

And yet it was not by rebellion but by creation that Wordsworth and Coleridge triumphed. How many times have young men, seemingly as clever and foolish as those two, hopefully sworn to

> "Run amuck
> With this old world for want of strife
> Sound asleep."

84

And how often has the poor sequel been

"No work done, but great works undone."

But those two actually performed all that they promised to each other upon the Quantock heaths. And the marvellous Coleridge did the greater part of his share in the revolution that very winter before they parted! For there and then he wrote *The Ancient Mariner* and the first part of *Christabel*. He wrote them to illustrate his new theory of poetry; how it should thrill men with tales of antique glamour. If more of us could just sit down and " illustrate " our new theories of literature as happily as Samuel Taylor on that occasion what a world it would be!

Wordsworth, on the other hand, proposed as the proper substitute for Pope something very different from a revival of mediæval supernaturalism. He aspired to give us the inner life of man in contemplation of nature. His mountain ash took a few years longer to grow to perfection than Coleridge's magic gourd. In the Quantocks the principal products of his Muse, according to his own account of it in the *Prelude*, were *Peter Bell* and *The Thorn*. There are fine passages in both poems, but both failed to show their author's full strength — not merely or even chiefly because they contained lines immortally absurd, like

"The Ass turned round his head and *grinned*,
Appalling process!"

and

"I've measured it from side to side:
'Tis three feet long, and two feet wide,"

—but for the larger reason that both poems contain too much of incident, glamour and violence, which assort ill with the true genius of Wordsworth. The fact was that, although he was writing to illustrate a principle opposed to Coleridge's theory, he was nevertheless for the moment too much under his friend's influence. But in those same months on the Quantocks he also wrote minor poems entirely in his own best manner: " I heard a thousand blended notes "; " It is the first mild day of March "; the last two lines of *Simon Lee*; and " Up! up! my friend, and quit your books." And he had scarcely left the Quantocks and Coleridge, in the summer of 1798, before he wrote the first of his masterpieces, *Tintern Abbey*. In the next half-dozen years followed nearly all his greatest work replete with " vital feelings of delight." He had in that short while done more for the happiness and perfection of mankind than all the Pantisocratic societies that ever talked. His poems dwell in us, while *The Ancient Mariner*, a greater miracle of art perhaps, is a tale told by a strange man from a far country. Mediæval magic is outside our daily experience — a recreation, not a sustenance; but Wordsworth's poems are the inner life we live if we are wise:

> " Under such banners militant, the soul
> Seeks for no trophies, struggles for no spoils
> That may attest her prowess, blest in thoughts
> That are their own perfection and reward,
> Strong in herself and in beatitude
> That hides her, like the mighty flood of Nile
> Poured from his fount of Abyssinian clouds
> To fertilize the whole Egyptian plain."

It is, then, more desirable than Mr Brandes thinks that the Truce of Poetry should be observed whenever the spirit of liberty can honestly exist without open rebellion. The best poetry should be the common ground of all creeds and of all parties. What a blessing it is that we do not know what " party " or " Church "—or no-Church—Shakespeare " belonged to "; while the innate conservatism of *Paradise Lost* so neatly balances Milton's Republicanism that he remains a national instead of a party asset. Poetry unites those whom all other writing divides. It is a body of scripture, almost a religion, common to those who, though not of one opinion in everything, seek some method by which to approach one another on subjects of deepest feeling and importance. Liberal spirits and pious souls would have greater difficulty in understanding each other if it were not for Milton, Wordsworth and Shelley, and the emotions to which they give the most perfect expression. If poetry were at all widely understood and loved, we should find among men more of those several qualities to engender which is the true function of religion and of free thought, of conservative and liberal movements.

For this reason, and for many others besides, there is truth in the old saying about the songs and the laws; yes, the songs of the people would indeed be more important than their laws, if only they learnt the songs and lived by them, as they learn and observe the laws! But how little is this condition fulfilled, even among us English, whose greatest achievement among so many great achievements is the body of poetry we have produced. Of how much real account is this heritage of ours in the spiritual life even of our educated class? What percentage of persons in any section of the community has read any poem of Shelley, Wordsworth or Keats twice through for love of it?

There is also another and potentially a vaster sphere of influence for our poets, in America, where, for thousands of years to come, innumerable millions will be brought up to speak our common tongue. Let us hope that at least some thousands of them in every generation may be endowed with the qualities of mind and spirit necessary to make Shakespeare and Milton, Wordsworth and Keats more to them than names of people whose houses are to be visited on tour. May these poets exert over us and our remote descendants the same enormous and enduring influence that Virgil and Dante exerted over old Europe. Otherwise, whatever successes may attend on Democracy or on Empire, the Anglo-Saxon race will have failed in its chief mission of spreading in widest commonalty the highest pleasures which the human spirit can enjoy.

# HISTORY AND FICTION

BEING PART OF THE SIDGWICK MEMORIAL LECTURE AT
NEWNHAM COLLEGE, CAMBRIDGE, 1921 [1]

HISTORICAL fiction is not history, but it springs from history
and reacts upon it. Historical novels, even the greatest of
them, cannot do the specific work of history; they are not
dealing, except occasionally, with the real facts of the past.
They attempt instead to create, in all the profusion and
wealth of nature, typical cases imitated from, but not
identical with, recorded facts. In one sense this is to make
the past live, but it is not to make the events live, and
therefore it is not history.

Historical fiction has done much to make history popular
and to give it value, for it has stimulated the historical imagination. Indeed, a hundred years ago it altered our whole
conception of the past, when Scott, by his lays and novels,
revolutionized history. He found it, in his boyhood, composed of two elements distinctive of eighteenth - century
thought—first, the patient antiquarianism that was laying
the foundations of history proper, and, secondly, a habit of
sententious generalization which, though much in advance
of the wholly unphilosophic historical gossip of preceding
ages, missed a number of the most important points for want
of sympathy and experience. " The age of common sense "
had forgotten, among other things, what a revolutionist or
a religious fanatic was really like.

This form of the historical art, with its sound antiquarianism and its superficial analysis, was already moribund,
having reached perfection under the hands of Gibbon.
For within its narrow limits something like perfection was
possible to this kind of history, and perfection cannot grow.

[1] Reprinted, with kind permission, from the *Cornhill Magazine*.

# HISTORY AND FICTION

No one could improve on Pope, so poetry stood still for fifty years, till Wordsworth gave it a fresh start. History had not so long to wait. For Scott followed on Gibbon so soon as to leave history no time to dawdle and decay, perched on the height where the great master had set it. Gibbon had traced in his cold, clear outline the procession of fourteen calamitous centuries, that move past us with slow and stately pace, each as like to the one that it follows as are the figures in the frieze of the Parthenon. That was how Scott found history; he left it what it has been ever since, an eager aspiration, destined to perpetual change, doomed to everlasting imperfection, but living, complex, broad as humanity itself.

To the calm eye of Gibbon mankind remained from the age of the Antonines to the age of Rienzi essentially the same, divided up in each succeeding era into a number of formulæ—the magistrates, the philosophers, the priests, the nobles, the plebeians, the barbarians—each class retaining the same generalized character throughout the piece. It was Sir Walter who first showed us how not only clothes and weapons, but thought and morals vary according to the period, the province, the class, the man. To him the pageant of history was more like a Walpurgis night than a Parthenon procession. His Shakespearean wealth of imagination and breadth of sympathy, furnished with ever fresh material from the mine of his antiquarian researches, answered more truly than Gibbon's classicism to the wild variety of nature, for ever making and breaking new types of men and things. The most famous lines of the poetry of Scott's own era, though I dare say Sir Walter thought them sad stuff, read like an ætherialized version of his own view of history:

" Worlds on worlds are rolling ever
From creation to decay
Like the bubbles on a river,
Sparkling, bursting, borne away.

But they are still immortal
Who, through birth's Orient portal
And death's dark chasm hurrying to and fro,
Clothe their unceasing flight
In the brief dust and light
Gathered around their chariots as they go.
New shapes they still may weave,
New gods, new laws, receive:
Bright or dim are they, as the robes they last
On death's bare ribs have cast."

Historians who came after Scott thought quite differently about the past from those who came before him. Macaulay, when he and the century were each twenty-eight years old, wrote an essay " On History " (now printed in his *Miscellaneous Writings*). The young essayist there sketched out the kind of history which he already aspired to write, and actually wrote twenty years later. He says: " Sir Walter Scott has used those fragments of truth which historians have scornfully thrown behind them. But a truly great historian would reclaim those materials which the novelist has appropriated." Now, if you will look to see what Hume, Robertson and Gibbon lack, you will see at once how very large are the " fragments of truth " that even the greatest historians " threw behind them " before Scott taught them better. Everything that is intimate, everything that is passionate, everything also that is of trivial or daily occurrence, all the colour and all the infinite variety of the past. It is not merely the " truly great historian," but the middle-sized and small historians whose sphere has been enlarged by the pioneer work and infectious example of Scott. But the great ones no doubt profited most greatly. Scott " fished the murex up," so that Carlyle outdid Macaulay in azure feats; " both gorged "; but Scott himself, we all rejoice to remember, managed to " eat turtle " for a while.

An historical novelist, if he is to be anything more than a boiler of the pot, requires two qualities: an historical mind apt to study the records of a period, and a power or creative imagination able to reproduce the perceptions so acquired in a picture that has all the colours of life. Some writers, like Charlotte Yonge, Charles Reade, Stanley Weyman, and Mr John Buchan, in his set of short historical tales, *The Path of the King*—perhaps the best thing he has written—can do valuable work, each in his own degree, by exploiting carefully the results of modern historical scholarship, with the help of the amount of imagination that each has.[1]

In some of the early historical novels of Sir Quiller Couch —*The Blue Pavilions*, for example, or *The Splendid Spur*— imagination plays the greater part. The historical setting, though not unscholarly, seems to have been chosen mainly as supplying an enfranchisement from the world of present-day reality for a young author who wished to let his humour and fancy run wild in the pastures. Yet he has enough of the historical sense to make the times of Charles I. or William III. serve very naturally the purposes of his freakish imagination.

Charles Kingsley and Mr Kipling both exercise a great effect in stimulating the imagination of young and old— Mr Kipling especially in this generation, brought up at the foot of Pook's Hill. Both men had the gift of imagination. Both succeeded in reproducing in the brightest living colours the social, political and military details, and the material scenery of the past. But they had a failing in common. Their actors are too modern in thought and motive. Kingsley's Saxon and Tudor heroes are, too patently, muscular Christians and Victorian gentlemen. Mr Kipling's Romans and Normans are " subs," fresh from Harrow and Sandhurst, engaged in saving the empire. But the fault of " modernizing " character and motive is to some degree unavoidable in writing novels about remote ages, because, when we cannot know what the people were really like, all

[1] Since this paragraph was written a new star of Historical Fiction has arisen—Mrs Naomi Mitchison.

we can do is to fashion substitutes out of our own modern experience. Now, although human nature is somewhat the same in all ages, we may be sure it was not so much the same as all that. The same praise and the same criticism may be passed on Mr Shaw's *St Joan*.

*Ivanhoe* is less like the Middle Ages than *Puck of Pook's Hill*, because when it was written even less was known about the period. But, in its day, *Ivanhoe* was the greatest single step towards opening out the Middle Ages to modern conception; for it was the first attempt to envisage our distant ancestors as human beings at all. And when we come to the Scottish novels of Scott and Stevenson, the fault of " modernizing " is much less marked. Scott and Stevenson in their most successful tales chose Scottish themes in periods sufficiently modern to allow the introduction of the language and character of the vigorous Scots whom they knew so well in daily life.

The thought, feelings and language of North Britain in the nineteenth century, when modified by the sound anti-quarian knowledge of Scott and Stevenson, do well enough in tales of Montrose, the Covenanters and Prince Charlie. For this reason Sir Walter's foot is safest on his native heath, and Stevenson's eighteenth-century Scottish stories, together with *St Ives* and his unfinished masterpieces, the *Heathercat* and *Weir of Hermiston*, succeed for the same reasons. Similarly Tolstoi transfers back the Russians he knew to the period of Napoleon, in what is, perhaps, the greatest of all historical novels, *War and Peace*.

Modern Cockney or provincial English characters and dialects can also be safely transferred back a century or so —as in the case of Mr Jerry Cruncher and his wife in *A Tale of Two Cities*, and Mr Rowley in Stevenson's *St Ives*. But they could hardly be transferred into the Middle Ages with much *vraisemblance*. And so in *The Black Arrow* and in the brilliantly coloured sketch called *The Sire de Maletroit's Door*, Stevenson, though he gives a most vivid and passably accurate picture of the state of society in the fifteenth century, is fain, like Mr Kipling, to fall back on modern or conventional motives and characters. In *A Lodging for the Night* Stevenson has the real character of Villon " given," out of Villon's own poems; and so the tale succeeds, even though it is laid as far back as France of the fifteenth century.

That tale of Mr Kipling which he has entitled *The Finest Story in the World* succeeds because it stops short on the threshold of the unknown. When the story breaks off sharp we wake with " immortal longings on us," as from an unfinished dream of strange passion and adventure, that we seemed to be on the point of enjoying, when it faded at cock-crow. This effect, artistically the highest but not capable of prolongation, has been sacrificed in *Puck of Pook's Hill*. There, in order to enjoy the supreme pleasure of living for some appreciable hours in a fully visible past, we gladly pay the price of partial disillusionment, which no oak, ash or thorn can magic away from grown-up eyes.

Thackeray's *Esmond* is one of the best of English historical novels, judged as such. Clearly it owes much to Macaulay. But it is the work of historical fiction in which a feeling for the spirit and details of a period in the past is most perfectly blended with the human interest. *Il y a des longueurs* even in *Esmond*, but these are not due to any failure with the historical setting. Hardy's *Dynasts* is the greatest work of historical fiction of our time. He is the only modern who has an epic quality.

Historical fiction proper looks backward by the help of imagination and antiquarian study. But there is another class of work which we may call " contemporary " historical fiction—that is, the epic, drama or novel of contemporary manners, which acquires historical value only by the passage of time. Just because Homer, Shakespeare and Fielding copied from the life of their own day, their work, as historical evidence, has a value entirely lacking to the historical novel proper.

They give evidence, not, indeed, as to particular events,

# HISTORY AND FICTION

but as to the manners, thought and customs which they knew so well, revealing just those psychological shades in which chronicles and legal or economic records are deficient.

At the head of the works of fiction that time has thus transformed into historical evidence stand Homer's lays. In a period of which we know otherwise almost nothing at all—far less than we know about the England of the Conquest—Homer has rendered the daily life and thought of those far-off men and women more familiar and intimate to us than are the lives of any of our English ancestors prior to the time of Chaucer. Homer gives us a glimpse through the blackest part of the " curtain of old night," into chambers hung with glittering armour and rocky coasts under a burning sun. Even " If the *Iliad* and *Odyssey* were all fiction," says Professor Gilbert Murray in that most imaginative and entrancing of works of scholarship, *The Rise of the Greek Epic*:

" If the *Iliad* and *Odyssey* were all fiction we should still learn from them a great deal about early Greek customs, about practices of war and government, about marriage, land tenure, worship, farming, commerce, and, above all, the methods of seafaring. Let anyone read thoughtfully the story which Eumæus the swineherd tells of his life, in *Odyssey* O. (xv.), and then consider how much history of the life of the Ægean, about the seventh century B.C., he has learnt from three pages of poetical fiction."

After Homer come Chaucer's Prologues and Tales and the Elizabethan theatre. We value Ben Jonson to-day less for his " learnèd sock " than for such learning as he shares with Hogarth and Charles Dickens, the things he saw and heard in the pothouses and alleys of old London, and reproduced with an art that only the author of Falstaff could surpass. Beaumont and Fletcher's *Knight of the Burning Pestle*, which links up Aristophanes with Gilbert and Sullivan, is " of so airy and light a quality " that, considered as historical evidence, many will hold it "but a shadow's shadow." And yet I think it helps to prove that the old 'prentice life of London once contained a spirit of lyrical joy and imagination not to be found in the city life of to-day.

The views, not only of ordinary readers, but of historical specialists, have been deeply affected by Smollett, Fielding and Miss Austen, as regards the manners of the squirearchy and other classes in South England in the early and late eighteenth century respectively. Galt's *Annals of the Parish* does a similar service in respect to Scotland under George III. Fielding and Miss Austen were both shrewd observers, but the police magistrate may have exaggerated and the lady may have minimized the coarseness of the society which they approached from two different angles of experience. But when allowance has been fully made for this, the chasm that divides Fielding's Squire Western from Miss Austen's polished gentlemen of the same county fifty years later remains a problem of importance to historians. It suggests an idea which other evidence confirms, that a real change took place among the rural gentry during the century that boasted for its chief object the civilizing of the neglected manners of mankind. Beau Nash, who operated as Master of the Ceremonies at Bath in the same county, was one of the chief leaders of the movement which improved away Squire Western.

The name of Bath reminds us how contemporary fiction, when it is great literature, usurps the place of history in our thoughts about the past. As the stones of Venice still embody the Italian Middle Age, so do the stones of Bath embody the English eighteenth century. The outward aspect of the town still reflects the character and breeding of those who gave it glory, the aristocracy, whose motto was "*simplex munditiis.*" Its comfortable and dignified streets, cast up the hillside in lavish disarray, received fashionable society, season after season, during the hundred years when fashionable society had taken over the conduct of politics and the patronage of letters and art from the fallen Court of the Kings, and had not yet handed them on to the people at large.

Under the first four Georges there is scarcely one of " the Great " to whom Bath was not familiar. Yet it is not their memory that most haunts us when we visit that city. Perhaps, indeed, as a phantom post-chaise turns the corner of the London Road, we can see through the window the profile of the dying Pitt with the Austerlitz look upon it. Perhaps at the Pump Room we may remember two of its extinct tyrants, Beau Nash and Dr Johnson. But most of us will think more often of certain much humbler West Country families who, judged by strictly historical standards, never existed at all. The spot in Bath that I was most anxious to identify was the room where Catherine first saw Tilney at the dance.

History can tell us comparatively little about people as humble as Catherine and Tilney. Yet Tilneys and Catherines were always more numerous than Dr Johnsons and Pitts, and they more closely resembled you and me. If the genius of Miss Austen can reveal their hearts and minds to us, our historical knowledge is immensely enlarged. She has not only written great psychological novels for all time; she has also enabled the people of the twentieth century to look back into the minds and hearts of their analogues in the last years of George III., in a manner entirely beyond the scope of the historian.

" Balzac's novels form the best history of 1830. He alone, among French historians, has grasped the essential features of the society that revolted from the ideas of the Restoration." [1] Those words are not mine. They were written by Professor York Powell, who also declared that " History is an absolute science, as much, for example, as botany." How he reconciled these two opinions I am not called upon to explain. At any rate, if, according to Powell, Balzac is an " historian," and if an " historian " (again according to

[1] Oliver Elton's *Life of York Powell*, i. 417.

Powell) equals a " scientist," and if, therefore, Balzac is a " scientist," then this much-debated question, whether or not history is a science, is the merest battle about words. For my part, though I do not think history is a mere science, I should not call Balzac an historian. But he has certainly left us a great historical document on France in the thirties.

Among our most priceless national archives are *Peter Simple* and *Midshipman Easy*. Their author—think of it!— had himself been a midshipman in Cochrane's ship the year after Trafalgar! What would we not give to have an equally vivacious collection of stories about the conquest of Gaul from the *stylus* of a real subaltern of Cæsar's Tenth Legion; or about the settlement of England dictated by a Norman lad who had come over the year after Hastings! Even if all the adventures were imaginary, how immensely our knowledge would be increased.

One of the many rewards for acquiring historical knowledge is the pleasure thereby added to our reading of the great works of fiction which are becoming historical by the passage of time. Their number is increasing year by year; already *Pickwick* and the Victorian novels—Trollope's, for example —are beginning to take on this character. Historical scholarship not only enables us to understand words and references scattered haphazard along the page, but adds to our enjoyment of the contemporary picture of bygone classes and types, each with its social, political or religious peculiarities, because we see it all in the setting of our knowledge of the whole period. When Squire Western says, " Most o' zuch great estates be in the hands of lords, and I heate the very name of themmum," the point of these words in the mouth of one of the richest landowners in Somersetshire is doubled if we are aware of the social and political relation of the Tory squirearchy of that day to the prevalently Whig Upper House. And when his prim sister, whose foible is affairs of State, says to him, " Brother, I am entirely at your service. Things look so well in the North that I was never in a better

HISTORY AND FICTION

humour," it gives us a perceptible glow of pleasure to be able to recognize in her chance expression " the North " the political jargon of the age, in which "the North " meant the group of foreign questions centring round Sweden. And in larger matters there is a real intellectual pleasure in comparing the aspects of society which struck or escaped the notice of contemporary novelists with the same or different phenomena emphasized by the retrospective analysis of modern social historians, such as Professor Clapham or Mr and Mrs Hammond, who, we may remark, more and more treat old novels as a form of evidence to be collated with other sources.

Meredith's *Vittoria* partakes of the character of both the classes of fiction which we have been discussing. It is partly an historical novel looking back to the past, like *Waverley* or *Westward Ho!*; partly a work of contemporary fiction that has by process of time become historical, like Chaucer or Miss Austen. The scene of *Vittoria* is laid in 1848, and is a study of the spirit of the *quarantotto*; but Meredith's knowledge of Italian patriots and Austrian officers, though firsthand, was of later date. He acquired it chiefly in the sixties, and his knowledge of the Austrians in particular he owed to his acting with them as war correspondent for *The Morning Post* in the Königgrätz campaign of 1866. *Vittoria* contains the finest and truest picture of Mazzini that has ever been drawn; it is the best appreciation of the Italian character in its strength and its weakness; and it is, I think, the best book ever written, either in prose or poetry, about the Italian *Risorgimento*, even though the last part of it "is lost in shallows and in miseries."

History and literature were regarded as sisters in the classical culture which ruled the European intellect for four hundred years and is now passing away. Under that regime both literature and history flourished in this island, and much else besides. What have we to put in its place? I hope we shall try to replace it by a modern culture in which history and literature will still be regarded as sisters. If not, it will fare ill with both of them. They will both be impoverished. They will, if isolated from one another, fail to appeal to the best intellects and highest imaginations which classical education attracted of old.

Fortunately the study of Modern Literature, as now conducted in schools and colleges, is entering into close relations with History. Teachers find that they cannot explain the poets and prosemen, even of the last century, without giving them an " historical background." To be rightly understood, Shelley and Byron are already in need of the prelude of the French Revolution and the environment of the Holy Alliance: their poems can no more be studied *in vacuo* than Milton and Chaucer themselves.

The flourishing Schools of English and of Mediæval and Modern Languages at Cambridge have felt increasingly the necessity of teaching the historical background of the literatures and languages which their pupils are studying. The best part of the old classical ideal of education—that is, the teaching of history and literature side by side—is, in fact, reviving in the modern field by force of its own merits.

In this connection I read with great interest Mr R. B. McKerrow's paper (in the English Association Pamphlets, No. 49) on the teaching of English language and literature, where he writes that students of English " need know little of the superficial kind of history which deals with wars and politics, but they *must* know something of the great changes in life and thought which accompanied and inspired the literature with which they are to deal." Literature, he says in effect, is closely connected in origin and spirit with the main religious, political, social and commercial currents of each age, and these must be known before the literature of the past can be fully understood and appreciated.

And if the study of literature thus requires an " historical background," most periods of civilized history have their " literary background," without which they lose a great part of their meaning and value as subjects of study. To take one example out of many, we should care little about the fascinating state of society in England in the eighteenth century if we were ignorant of its literary and classical atmosphere, that lent to Chatham's genius its majestic eloquence, and mingled even the tainted breeze of political corruption with a perfume so delicious.

There is another way in which history and literature are allied. At bottom, the motive that draws men and women to study history is poetic. It is the desire to feel the reality of life in the past, to be familiar with " the chronicle of wasted time " for the sake of " ladies dead and lovely knights "—if it were only by discovering the nature of the "lovely knights'" fees. History starts out from this astonishing proposition—that there is no difference in degree of reality between past and present. Lady Jane Grey was once as actual as anyone in this room. And we had best be careful before we think of her as a phantom lady with her head under her arm, for we are of her succession, and shall soon be no more and no less ghostly than she. We, too, are only queens and kings for a day. We are all food for history. No one century, not even the twentieth, is more real than any other. That is the most obtrusive and hackneyed, and yet the most mysterious, of all facts. It is the common ground of all religions, all philosophies, all poetry. Though some of us may think of it this way and some that, it is at the bottom of all our thinking.

The Elizabethan poets were obsessed by it. They called it "mortality," and have given to it the most profound and beautiful expression in all literature:

> " Since brass, nor stone, nor earth, nor boundless sea,
> But sad mortality o'ersways their power;
> How with his rage shall beauty hold a plea,
> Whose action is no stronger than a flower? "

Hamlet in the graveyard was more concerned with the fact

that we would soon all be as dead as Alexander and Yorick
than with the more consoling proposition that Alexander
and Yorick had once been as much alive as we. It is that
more cheerful side of the matter which history labours to
make real to our slow imaginations. The past is a tale of
real people, not of abstractions. To this poetic philosophy,
inherent in every smallest historical fact, Carlyle has again
and again given expression. Though he often, indeed,
groaned over Dry-as-dust, he idealized his work, and even
went so far as to prefer the smallest fact about the past that
Dry-as-dust could collect, as being more poetical than all
Shelley and more romantic than all Scott. Take any passage
at random from *Past and Present*:

"But now, sure enough, at Waltham 'on the second
Sunday of Quadragesima,' which Dryasdust declares to
mean the 22nd day of February, year 1182, thirteen St
Edmundsbury Monks are, at last, seen processioning towards the Winchester Manor House; and, in some high
Presence Chamber and Hall of State, get access to Henry II.
in all his glory. What a Hall—not imaginary in the least,
but entirely real and indisputable, though so extremely
dim to us; sunk in the deep distances of Night! The Winchester Manor House has fled bodily, like a Dream of the
old Night; not Dryasdust himself can show a wreck of it.
House and people, royal and episcopal, lords and varlets,
where are they? Why, *there*, I say, seven centuries off;
sunk *so* far in the Night, there they *are*; peep through the
blanket of the old Night, and thou wilt see!"

And then, in the description of the sudden breaking off
of the Monk Jocelin's chronicle, we have a passage that
goes to the very root of the magic that lurks in every original
document:

"The magnanimous Abbot makes preparation for departure; departs, and—And Jocelin's Boswellian Narrative,
suddenly shorn through by the scissors of Destiny, *ends*.
There are no words more; but a black line, and leaves
of blank paper. Irremediable; the miraculous hand, that

held all this theatric machinery, suddenly quits hold; impenetrable Time-curtains rush down; in the mind's eye all is again dark, void; with loud dinning in the mind's ear, our real phantasmagory of St Edmundsbury plunges into the bosom of the twelfth century again, and all is over. Monks, Abbot, Hero-worship, Government, Obedience, Cœur-de-Lion, and St Edmund's shrine, vanish like Mirza's vision; and there is nothing left but a mutilated black ruin amid green botanic expanses, and oxen, sheep and *dilettanti* pasturing in their places."

And, again, in that most wonderful essay of his on Boswell's *Johnson* he says:

" Consider all that lies in that one word *Past*! What a pathetic, sacred, in every sense *poetic*, meaning is implied in it; a meaning growing ever the clearer, the farther we recede in time—the *more* of that same *Past* we have to look through! History after all is the true poetry. And Reality, if rightly interpreted, is greater than Fiction."

Intellectually, of course, everyone would always admit that the past was real—with the exception of a few metaphysicians who might claim to reserve judgment on the point. But to admit the truth of the proposition is not to feel it as a living fact. It is the detailed study of history that makes us feel it; that is the attracting pleasure of this study, which inspires the driest of antiquarians and the most scientific of historians. The ignorant Philistine thinks that we historians are absorbed in the dusty records of the dead; he supposes we can see nothing save:

" The lost-to-light ghosts, grey-mailed,
    As you see the grey river mist
    Holds shapes on the yonder bank."

But to us, as we read, they take form, colour, gesture, passion, thought. It is only by study that we can see our forerunners, remote and recent, in their habits as they lived, intent each on the business of a long-vanished day, riding out to do homage or to poll a vote; to seize a neighbour's manor-house and carry off his ward, or to leave cards on ladies in crinolines.

And there in the field, generation after generation, is the ploughman behind the oxen, the horses, the machine, and his wife busy all day in the cottage, waiting for him with her daily accumulated budget of evening news.

Each one, gentle and simple, in his commonest goings and comings, was ruled by a complicated and ever-shifting fabric of custom and law, society and politics, events at home and abroad, some of them little known by him and less understood. Our effort is not only to get what few glimpses we can of his intimate personality, but to reconstruct the whole fabric of each passing age, and see how it affected him; to get to know more in some respects than he himself knew about the conditions that enveloped and controlled his life.

There is nothing that more divides civilized from semi-savage man than to be conscious of our forefathers as they really were, and bit by bit to reconstruct the mosaic of the long-forgotten past. To weigh the stars, or to make ships sail below the sea, is not a more astonishing and ennobling performance on the part of the human race in these latter days than to know the course of events that had been long forgotten, and the true nature of men and women who were here before us. Truth is the criterion of historical study; but its impelling motive is poetic. Its poetry consists in its being true. Work that out and you will get a synthesis of the scientific and literary views of history.

# ENGLISHMEN AND ITALIANS

SOME ASPECTS OF THEIR RELATIONS PAST AND PRESENT [1]

I PROPOSE this afternoon to analyse some of the causes of the close friendship existing between Italians and Englishmen sixty years ago. That friendship helped the creation of United Italy, and thereby led to the fortunate participation of the new state in the war of our own day.

The Italian policy of Lord John Russell is a striking exception to the general failure or misdirection of our foreign policy in the middle nineteenth century. That exceptional success was due to the fact that Italy was the only country in Europe or America about which we English in the middle of the nineteenth century were really well informed. Our ignorance, happily since dispelled, both of the American Republic and of the Turkish Empire, dictated our official attitude to those two states respectively at the time of the Crimea, the American Civil War, and Disraeli's defence of the Turk. But during those very decades our statesmen and our public had an intimate and personal knowledge of Italy answering in extent and closeness of sympathy to our knowledge of America to-day. And this knowledge was the reason why our Italian policy was so successful and so wise, in an epoch when our other dealings with the outer world were a series of well-meant blunders.

In order to analyse the character and conditions of this remarkable friendship, closer at that time than any perhaps which has ever bound two nations not kin by blood, we ought first to survey a long vista of English cultural history. For the interest of our grandfathers in Italy drew its origin from their inherited cultural associations, from their passionate and many-sided devotion to the literature, language, art, history, and civilization of ancient, of mediæval, and of

[1] Read before the British Academy, June 1919.

modern Italy. English sympathy with the cause of the South American republics in the days of Canning had been commercial and political; but the sympathy of the next generation for the Italian cause was cultural and political, answering in that respect to the Byronic sympathy with Greece, but far more profound, personal, and well informed.

I must lightly pass over the long and fascinating history of the cultural relations of England and Italy from the time of Julius Cæsar to the eighteenth century—those eighteen hundred years of the ebb and flow of civilization. That great argument is mainly the story of England's debt to Italy—a debt she can never repay. One main cause of divergence between the history of England and the history of Germany has lain in the fact that although the English race is mainly Teutonic and Scandinavian in origin, yet we derive ultimately from Italian sources so many of the words in our language and most of the form and a portion of the spirit of our literature.

England's debt to Italy, in the elements that have formed our own civilization, derives from three sources: *First*, what we got direct from ancient Rome either in language, law, religion, art, or political ideas, and in the study of the Latin classics, renewed from age to age down to our own day. *Secondly*, what we got from France, and therefore indirectly from Italy, since French civilization was Roman in origin; this French influence was the formative element in English civilization in Norman and Plantagenet times. *Thirdly*, and lastly, what English literature took direct from the great Italian civilization of the later Middle Ages and the Renaissance period. From the time of Chaucer onwards we abandoned the native Anglo-Saxon literature of alliterative verse, like *Piers Plowman*, adapting the English language to French and Italian forms of verse and prose; while our writers borrowed what were mainly Italian themes. Chaucer took many of his stories from Boccaccio, though he improves them in the telling. Nearly half the personages of Shakespeare's dramas bear Italian names; even Hamlet's friend in what is supposed to be the tenth-century Court of Denmark must needs be called Horatio, and when he wants to commit suicide he tells us he is more an antique Roman than a Dane. Shakespeare's good and bad dukes and their courtiers are all derived from the little Italian Courts of the Renaissance period, held in such cities as Mantua, Milan and Urbino, when Italy was to England "the glass of fashion and the mould of form." A generation later Milton used to compose not only in Latin but in Italian, and saw no difference between ancient Italy and the Italy of his own day as seen from the altitude of Parnassus. He was a friend of Galileo; and our scientific men of that century down to Newton were in constant correspondence with the scientific men of Italy, who were in no small degree their masters.

It is perhaps in the sphere of political institutions that the English have been most original in their native invention, from the time of Magna Charta downwards, or even from the time of William the Conqueror. Certainly it is in politics that the world at large has borrowed most from us; for our literature, though as great as the Greek or Latin, has had relatively little influence outside the English-speaking nations. In politics modern Italy, under Cavour, went to school in England, borrowing thence her constitutional monarchy and parliament. Yet even in the realm of political ideas, where we have taught more than we learned, how much we owed to Ancient Rome! The Conservative idea of respect for law and of the sovereign regal power was throughout our history sanctioned by the glamour of classical association hanging round the words *Lex, Rex, Imperator*. Our Plantagenet and our Tudor foundations were built on the Roman model. And no less in the realm of Liberal thought, the ideal of Roman Republican virtue, perpetuated in Livy, Plutarch, and Tacitus, did as much to inspire Milton, Sidney, and the opponents of the Stuarts as the Old Testament itself. How does Milton address a leading politician of the Commonwealth?—

" Vane, young in years but in sage counsel old,
  Than whom a better senator ne'er held
  The helm of Rome, when gowns, not arms, repelled
The fierce Epirot and the African bold."

Indeed, when Puritanism waned, and Whiggism took its place as the standard-bearer of the Liberty of the Subject, Brutus and Cato more and more replaced Ehud and Jael—on the whole a refinement—as examples for a modern civilized state.

Nay, more! The whole English conception of "patriotism" that embraces our Conservative and our Liberal ideas in one, and adds a something that transcends them both—this idealized English patriotism was in some measure the outcome of countless generations of English schoolboys studying the models of Roman antiquity. That spirit of the mute English schoolboy imbibing patriotism from the history of Rome was finally given tongue in Macaulay's *Horatius* and *Lake Regillus*. The very word " patriot "—whether in its usual sense of a lover of his country, or in its seventeenth- and eighteenth-century use of a popular opponent of the Government—carries the mind back to Regulus, Cincinnatus and " the honourable men whose daggers did stab Cæsar." Such were its associations in the minds of our ancestors who first employed the word in English.

In our own day classics have been dethroned without being replaced. But throughout the seventeenth, eighteenth and nineteenth centuries our statesmen were so brought up that they thought of Rome as the hearth of their political civilization, where their predecessor Cicero had denounced Catiline; where the models of their own eloquence and statecraft, as taught them at Eton, Harrow and Winchester, had been practised and brought to perfection. And, therefore, the ruins of the Forum were as familiar, as sacred, and as moving to Russell and to Gladstone as to Mazzini and Garibaldi themselves. This was a prime fact in the history of the *Risorgimento*.

But before I come to the *Risorgimento*, I must say a word

# ENGLISHMEN AND ITALIANS

about the eighteenth-century England from which the Victorian age derived its belief in the primacy of things Italian. In the eighteenth century Italy as a nation lay dead after a slavery of two hundred years to foreigners, priests and petty despots. But she lived in the eternal life of her peasants; in her music, then dominant in Europe; in a few poets, a few men of science, and in the supreme genius of Piranesi, who represented her, only too truly, as a land of gigantic ruins overgrown by verdure and crawled under by monks, beggars and *dilettanti*. Yet such as she was, such as Piranesi drew her, she interested the English more than Germany or any other land save France. Her ruins were infinitely venerable to men whose culture was only too narrowly based on the classics, but whose range of travel did not extend to the isles of Greece, still buried deep in the filth of Turkish occupation. It was in the natural order of things that Gibbon, the most characteristic figure of that period of English civilization, should choose for his theme a thousand years of Italian history, as he sat amid the ruins of the grandeur that was Rome, listening with contemptuous melancholy to the dirge of the barefooted friars.

The Grand Tour that put the crown on an English gentleman's education included in those days France and Italy *de rigueur*, and any other country thrown in according to fancy as a bad third. To Horace Walpole and his contemporaries travelling in Italy meant, not the company of fellow-tourists in cosmopolitan hotels, but the hospitality of the little Courts and of the native aristocracy—a social life decadent indeed, but thoroughly Italian, centring on the opera, masked balls and the life of antiquarian *cognoscenti* and *virtuosi*. To the Englishman who stayed at home, art meant Italian pictures and Græco-Roman sculpture and ruined temples; from Claude onwards Italy was the Mecca of landscape painters. Music, once native English, had become Italian. Literature—outside Chaucer, Shakespeare and Milton, with their perpetual references to Italy—meant the classics, the French writers and the Italian poets. Not

108

only Dante, but Petrarch, Tasso, and finally Alfieri, were widely familiar in the original, particularly to ladies, in whose education modern Italian took the place of the virile Latin. In short, the educated English, when the French Revolution broke out, owed at least as much to Italy as to France, and there was no third rival.

I have recently been reading the letters of the Whig statesmen of that period, the men from whom Lord John Russell received in apostolic succession his love of Italy and his love of freedom. In the correspondence of Charles Fox and Lord Holland in 1796, while the young Buonaparte was overrunning the Italian fields, occur several letters written in very choice Italian, in which the two statesmen discuss the rival merits of various Italian authors and poets. And a third in that same set of men, Earl Grey, who afterwards passed the great Reform Bill, has left in his own handwriting a copy of a translation which he made of *The Banks of Allan Water*:

> " Dell' Adige sul lido
> Isaura m'incontrò,
> Dei fiori di Primavera
> Ornata e bella andò.
> La cercò un cavaliero
> Giurando eterno amor,
> Sull' Adige non era
> Donna più lieta ancor."

And so forth. Well, times have changed. I do not suppose that Mr Balfour and Viscount Grey, let alone Mr Lloyd George and Mr Bonar Law, are in the habit of writing to each other in Italian. Nor do I know which of our statesmen will undertake an Italian translation of *Allan Water*!

This, then, was the culture, based upon Italian things, ancient and modern—a culture limited, indeed, but profound and noble—which Shelley and Byron, Russell and Gladstone, the Brownings and Meredith, and all the English friends of Italy in the day of her resurrection inherited from the eighteenth century, and amplified with their own genius and with the Ruskinian learning of the new age. I do not say that that is why England sympathized with the Italian cause, for she sympathized also with the Polish cause; but it is the reason why her sympathy was not only passionate but constant, intimate, well informed and wisely directed.

The ideas and armies of the French Revolution came into Italy under the leadership of a man of Italian origin, a "prince" of the spiritual stock of Macchiavelli and the Borgias. Napoleon, not very tenderly but most effectually, raised his mother Italy, still but half-conscious, out of the death-trance of two centuries. For half-a-generation he gave her rational and modern government. The old petty despotisms were swept away, and the greater part of the peninsula was governed as if it were a nation, subject, indeed, to the Napoleonic French Empire, but as the Italian province thereof. The *Code Napoléon* instead of mediæval laws; efficient bureaucracy instead of the arbitrary whims of decadent tyrants by right divine; modern education on scientific and military lines instead of clerical obscurantism; the encouragement of the professional and middle classes on the principle of *carrière ouverte aux talents*, instead of caste privilege—such was the Napoleonic system by which Italians were educated to become capable in the next generation of rebellion on their own behalf, and ultimately of self-government.

The advent of the young Napoleon into Italy was hailed by Ugo Foscolo, the first poet of the actual *Risorgimento*, as the advent of Liberty herself. In his ode to *Buonaparte Liberatore*, in May 1797, he wrote:

" Ma tu dell' Alpi dall' äerie cime  
Al rintronar di trombe e di timballi  
Ausonia guati e giù piombi col volo.

. . . . . .

Gallia intuona e diffonde  
Di Libertade il nome  
E mare e cielo Libertà risponde."

Foscolo's poems are titanic and grandiose, suited to their age and subject. They reflect the appalling chiaroscuro of the French Revolutionary and Napoleonic epochs — when the light of new vast hopes for the rapid perfecting of the human race and the return of the Golden Age played on the surface of Cimmerian darkness, and, if they did not cure, at least revealed the horror of the world's old cruelty and law of force. " Shadows of prophecy shiver along by the lakes and the rivers and mutter across the ocean."

Ugo Foscolo was far indeed from remaining an uncritical admirer of Napoleon. It was he who said to John Cam Hobhouse: " Napoleon's dominion was like a July day in Egypt—all clear, brilliant, and blazing; but all silent, not a voice heard, the stillness of the grave."

Leipsic restored the *ancien régime* in Italy, and Waterloo ensured it for a generation to come. In 1816 Ugo Foscolo sought refuge in England — the first in that long roll of honour of the Italian exiles in our country. He was Italy's first unofficial representative, though his temperament was decidedly not diplomatic. He familiarized the Whig *salons* with the Italian aspirations—a new world of old romance peculiarly fitted, as I have shown, to arouse the sympathy of those learned, leisured and liberal aristocrats. With him begins the long line of friendships between Italian patriots and influential English men and women, that undirected and unsubsidized propaganda which for two generations to come slowly prepared the decisive diplomatic events of 1859 and 1860. Italians in England and Englishmen in Italy both laboured at this vocation—the former were founded by Foscolo, the latter by Shelley and Byron.

The first fifteen years after Waterloo, before Mazzini had fused the national discontent into a positive purpose with an aim ahead, were years of mere anger and despair. One great Italian and two great English poets have immortalized this dark moment in Italian history.

Leopardi, the contemporary of Shelley and Byron, is the

poet of despair, as befitted a subject of the Pope in that dreadful epoch between Napoleon's fall and Mazzini's rise:

> " Ahi troppo tardi
> E nella sera dell' umane cose
> Acquista oggi chi nasce il moto e il senso."

> (" Alas! too late,
> And in the evening tide of human things
> The child who's born to-day must move and feel.")

In that despair, utterly irremediable as it was for Leopardi's own soul, how much hope lay for Italy! Such despair, which had never been felt in the easy-going eighteenth century, was a measure of the work that Napoleon had done for Italy. He had saved her from being ever again content under the *mali governi*. Leopardi, in addressing his sister on the occasion of her marriage in 1821, used these terrible words:

> " O miseri, o codardi
> Figliuoli avrai, miseri eleggi."

> (" O, my sister, thou must needs bear children to be either unhappy or cowardly; choose, then, the unhappy.")

That epigram sums up the spirit of the Italian martyrdom of the generation that followed. The blank choice between misery and cowardice was nobly made by many Italians in every corner of the land.

There is a difference between the pessimism of Leopardi and the pessimism of some others. For his despair is not that of a man posing to the public, or denying virtue that he may enjoy vice, but of a man most terribly in earnest. It is significant that Mr Gladstone, at once the most optimistic and the most Christian of statesmen, should have felt for Leopardi, the denier, an admiration which he would never have extended to a spirit that had not some kinship with his own. No doubt he recognized that Leopardi's contempt for the life of man as he saw it lived in the territories of the Pope was not the pessimism that discourages from action and from virtue, but the cry of rage that may awaken the souls of the sleepers. And so indeed it proved.

During the years of Leopardi's lonely pain, Italy harboured two strangers who, like him, mourned over the ruins not only of Italian art and greatness, but of Italian freedom. But Byron and Shelley were true " children of the forcible isle," by no means inclined to sit down in despair. When, in 1820, the *Carbonari* of Naples rose in arms and forced a constitution on their Bourbon king, the hopes of the poets rose high. Shelley wrote the *Ode to Naples* in honour of the awakening of Italian liberty. The Austrian armies, who seemed to his imagination

> " Earth-born Forms
> Arrayed against the ever-living gods,"

marched down by order of the Holy Alliance through the length of Italy, suppressed the Neapolitan constitution, and conducted just such another cruel persecution of the best men of the professional and educated classes as had been conducted under Nelson's ægis more than twenty years before. But on this occasion England stood apart as neutral. The day was coming when she would be on the right side, and that day was prepared by the zeal with which Byron took up the Italian cause. For, in spite of the outcries of his respectable fellow-countrymen against him, the outcast sinner exerted even over them " an influence more than episcopal."

Byron discovered and assimilated into his own life the best as well as the worst that was doing in his land of exile. If intimacy with Italians proved his bane in Venice, it was his soul's salvation next year at Ravenna. He joined himself to the *Carbonari*—the vigorous and warlike peasants and gentlemen of the Romagna—the fathers of the men who saved Garibaldi in 1849—who were themselves, as early as 1821, conspiring to throw off the degrading yoke of the

Papal Government. Byron made practical preparations to fight, and if necessary to die, with his Italian friends, in case, as he most earnestly hoped, the rebellion at Naples should spread to the Romagna. Nothing but the too easy suppression of the south by the Austrian troops sent him to die for Greece instead of Italy.

"To-day," he writes on 18th February 1821, " I have had no communication with my Carbonari cronies; but in the meantime my lower apartments are full of their bayonets, fusils, cartridges, and what not. I suppose that they consider me as a depot, to be sacrificed, in case of accidents. It is no great matter, supposing that Italy could be liberated, who or what is sacrificed. It is a grand object—the very *poetry* of politics. Only think—a free Italy ! ! !"

Here was the splendid side of Byron, which more than redeems so much egoism, foppery and vice. He was the first Englishman who saw, in those dark days, that the Italians had a cause and a purpose of their own. Divesting himself in their company of his English prejudice, he lent these poor people his powerful aid, and was only too willing to give them a life which others of his countrymen, had they possessed his wealth, fame and genius, would certainly have valued more highly than to make a present of it to Romagnole peasants or Greek bandits. The new fact that a living Italy was struggling beneath the outward semblance of Metternich's " order " was thus perceived by Byron first of Englishmen, and by the " pard-like Spirit, beautiful and swift," who moved at his side through the Italian cities.

And so it was a mere chance that Byron died for Greece instead of for Italy. The Greek revolution is comparable to the Italian in this, that English sympathy with Greece against Turkey, which took effect at Navarino in 1872, arose mainly from cultural sentiment. It is true that the personal connections of Englishmen with Greece were feeble, while with Italy they were strong. The Greeks of that day were a distant and barbarous people. There was then no

Venezelos to speak the word of might. But the glamour of the mere name of Greece, coupled with that of Byron, sufficed to turn the England of Canning against Turkey on the Greek question, whereas we remained obstinately pro-Turk on the Bulgarian, Serbian and Armenian questions until 1880, in spite of the continual warnings of Bright and the belated but heroic crusade of Gladstone. This dual aspect of our relations with Turkey—pro-Greek, but anti-Bulgarian, anti-Serbian and anti-Armenian—proves that the sentiments aroused by the classical education of the day was really stronger with the upper-class churchgoers than the religion they professed. In nineteenth-century England, Christian sympathies, when it came to the point, were less strong than cultural sympathies evoked by the name of Hellas, since for fifty years after Navarino we enabled the Turks to continue to oppress and massacre the "barbarian" Christians who could not boast the magic name of Hellenes. We have wiped out that score at last, but at what a cost, on the heights of Gallipoli!

And yet our cultural and personal connections with modern Greece were very slender as compared to the ever fresh links binding us to the Italian patriots. Our personal knowledge of the Greeks practically ceased after Navarino, and we knew nothing at all of the Slav Christians buried in the Balkan Peninsula. This want of the kind of information that personal connections alone can give, accounts for our support of Turkish tyranny during the years that we were championing Italian freedom. In the Balkans and Armenia we knew not what we did in supporting the Turk, though in Italy we knew very well what Austria was doing. When there is no knowledge in the public here at home, when there are no personal and cultural links between England and the country in question, then and then only a single diplomat like Stratford de Redcliffe, or a single statesman of genius like Disraeli, can misdirect the policy of a great and honestly meaning empire. It has happened in the past. It will happen in the future, unless English people

# ENGLISHMEN AND ITALIANS

will seriously and affectionately study foreign lands. It is not safe to depend on a single " expert," official or unofficial. Experts who sympathize with some particular racial movement, though always enlightening, are usually one-sided. Out of the mouth of many witnesses only is the truth evinced. We need a great variety of connections of all sorts with all the nations of the world. We can no longer, as in the Victorian age, stand apart from the affairs of Europe whenever we wish. That happy independence is lost to us for ever, and if our only preparation for the new and heavy obligations of the coming era is to stop learning German, then indeed we are in evil case.

The drama of the great Italian effort of 1848-1849 has received more attention in English literature than any other phase of the Italian *Risorgimento*. Our poets and our great poetical novelist have not merely sung its praises, but have analysed and criticized the strength and weakness of the *quarantotto* with insight such as the writers of one country seldom have shown into the affairs of another. Meredith's *Vittoria* is not only a great prose poem on an epic moment in human affairs, but a detailed and accurate analysis of a people and of a period. Most historical novels are composed at second hand, out of history-books, but *Vittoria* sprang fully armed from Meredith's living knowledge of the primary authorities—Italian patriots and Austrian officers. The character of the revolution in the plain of the Po, which alone made the movement in the peninsula a serious fact, is better studied in *Vittoria* than in any history.

The feebler purpose of the Tuscan revolution of the same year, and the tragedy of the Tuscan character to which it led, is sympathetically yet mercilessly described in Mrs Browning's *Casa Guidi Windows*, whence she and her husband watched the rise and betrayal of liberty in 1848-1849. The contemporary comments of the poetess bear the stamp of wisdom and foresight even at this distance of time.

Garibaldi's defence of Rome in '49 was witnessed by Arthur Clough, the most cool and sceptical of men who ever possessed the warm, loving heart of a poet. Being on the spot, Clough, for all his habit " not to admire," could not guard himself against an invasion of passionate sympathy for Garibaldi and the "poor little Roman Republic." He threw his doubts, indignations and enthusiasm on the Roman question first into his own letters to his friends, and then into the epistolary hexameters of "Claude" in the *Amours de Voyage*. That poem—the amours excepted—is an exact replica of the real experiences of one of the most interesting tourists who ever visited Rome, and who chanced to be there at the most thrilling moment witnessed by the Eternal City in modern times.

During the decade of repression that followed 1849, the darkness before dawn, sympathy with the cause of the suffering Italians became general in England among whole classes who prior to 1848 had been ignorant, indifferent or hostile. The feeling for Italy spread from the poets to the Philistines. The desire to help Italy affected English middle-class politics so seriously that in the General Election and the Parliamentary proceedings of 1859 it was regarded as one of the chief reasons for the fall of the Derby Cabinet.

Then, as in the eighteenth century, the primacy of things Italian was maintained in men's thoughts through education, art and letters to a much greater extent than to-day. Music was still Italian more than German; and the opera, like everything else that was vital in Italy, had now become patriotic. "*Viva Verdi!*" was the cry of the musical world of that day; and Italian music masters were careful to explain to their pupils that its initials meant, being interpreted, "Viva Vittoria Emanuele Re d'Italia!"; the thought that one would cry "*Viva Verdi!*" under the noses of the Austrian police introduced a thrill of delicious romance into the music lessons of many an English miss. Italy, too, was still as great a centre of art as Paris itself. Before photography and other methods of reproduction had been perfected, great numbers of English painters were employed in copying pictures in the Italian churches and museums, particularly at Rome. And in original painting, too, Italy was the fashion. The wild mountain scenery of Calabria, and its operatic brigands, with their cone-shaped hats bedecked with ribbons of many colours, were for some reason the "right thing" in art then; and many adventurous young artists besides Edward Lear travelled and sketched in the strange and rugged lands that stretch beyond Vesuvius and Paestum for two hundred miles, whither few nowadays ever penetrate even with the motor-car to help. The friendship of English artists with Italians, and their devotion to the land and the people, was one of the many personal and cultural links that taught England to understand Italy. Costa's two friends, Sir Frederick Leighton and Lord Carlisle, were soaked in the spirit of Italy, as Du Maurier was soaked in the spirit of France. To Lord Carlisle's memories of those great days I have been indebted for much pleasant insight into by-paths of the *Risorgimento*.

In history and literature the connections of the two countries were as strong as in painting and music. Italian, not German, was still the foreign language learnt next after French. English ladies still read the modern and mediæval Italian poets. English gentlemen still enjoyed an education narrowly classical. And classical scholars, as compared with those of our time, were more interested in Rome and less in Greece. Virgil and Cicero were still in vogue. The Vatican sculptures and Pompeii were the goal of such as would now pass on to the Parthenon and to Delphi, to Crete and to Egypt. If foreign travel was less common than to-day, it was more concentrated upon Italy; and the charm of her landscapes and cities became associated in sympathetic English minds with the cause of the inhabitants of the country. Indeed, it was impossible to visit the peninsula without seeing clear signs of an odious oppression. Meanwhile, in England many of the best Italians of a great Italian era were congregated in exile, living on terms of close social intercourse with our chief political and literary families. Mazzini, Panizzi, Saffi, Poerio, Lacaita, and many others, enjoyed the personal affections of their English hosts as no other body of refugees ever did before or since. The important and startling conversion of Mr Gladstone to the Italian cause in 1851, no less than the warm attachment to that cause of Lord John Russell, of the Brownings, and of Tennyson, can be clearly traced to these conditions of literature and scholarship, of society and travel.

British sentiment in favour of Italian liberty, favoured by these general causes, was further enhanced when the patriotic movement in Italy ceased to be republican and became associated with the parliamentary monarchy of Victor Emmanuel of Piedmont, so ably developed by Cavour in acknowledged imitation of the English system.

The tide of sympathy for the Italian cause ran high, when, in 1859, a cross-current for a few months distracted and bewildered British opinion. Napoleon III. undertook to liberate North Italy from Austria, and marched his armies into the Lombard plain, in alliance with Victor Emmanuel's Piedmontese. Now, our grandfathers had one sentiment as strong as their sympathy with Italy, and that was their fear of France. England foresaw with terror the opening of another era of Napoleonic conquest, and it was with divided sympathies that she watched the Lombard campaign.

This confusion of the English mind on the subject of the war of 1859 was satirized by Matthew Arnold in *Friendship's Garland*, and by Ruskin in *Arrows of the Chase*. It would not be untrue to say that Englishmen hoped the Austrians would beat the French, and that the Piedmontese would beat the Austrians. What net result they wished to come out of the war they would scarcely have been able to explain; but the result that actually emerged was admirably suited to fulfil English wishes and to promote English policy.

The battles of Magenta and Solferino liberated Lombardy from Austria, and rendered the liberation of the rest of Italy possible in the near future. But the sudden termination of the campaign by the disappointing Treaty of Villa-franca ended the honeymoon of France and Italy, and threw Italy into the arms of England. The new Liberal Government, with Lord John Russell as Foreign Minister, was not slow to seize the opportunity. English interests were served by the disinterested feeling for the Italian cause prevailing over here, to which there was very little corresponding in French public opinion except in one corner of Napoleon's own heart. The English Press took up the cause of United Italy, pointed out to the Italians that Napoleon was but a half-hearted friend, and began to idolize Garibaldi as the enemy of Napoleon and of Austria alike. Cavour let England and France bid against each other for Italy's favour, and seized the opportunity, with Garibaldi's help, to make the Italian kingdom.

The action of Lord John Russell as Foreign Minister in 1860, backed as it was by an enthusiastic and well-informed public opinion, was one of the factors without which not even Cavour could have made Italy, for all the other Great Powers were opposed to Italian unity. I am here only concerned with those events so far as to show that they went right because Englishmen in general, and English ministers in particular, were thoroughly conversant with Italian affairs. Palmerston had not made a success of our Italian policy in 1848-1849; he had little understanding of the various movements in the peninsula, Venice and Sicily, though he displayed a wholesome and outspoken dislike of the despotic Governments. But in 1860 Lord John Russell and Mr Gladstone—to whom, especially to Russell, the right conduct of our policy was due—had for several years past been keen students of the Italian problem. It is only fair to add that in 1860 Palmerston, as Prime Minister, backed them up heartily. But the initiative in every step lay with Russell, coached from Italy by Hudson. The rest of the Cabinet, with less interest in Italy, merely submitted to the decrees of Palmerston, Russell and Gladstone, who were known as " the Italian *Triumvirate*."

Gladstone had first taken up the Italian cause not because he was a Liberal, but in spite of the fact that he was a Conservative, and greatly to the embarrassment of his then Conservative colleagues like Lord Aberdeen. The root of Gladstone's conversion is found in the cultural associations that had given him his first interest in Italy, and his consequent personal knowledge of the land and the people. In 1848, before he studied the question, he had been hostile to the Italian cause, and he would have remained so for a great many years longer if he had not, when on a holiday visit to Naples in the winter of 1850-1851, been induced by Lacaita to inspect the prisons there, and to attend the political trials in Bomba's law courts. That is not the sort of way our statesmen usually spend their holidays, even when they spend them on the Continent. And it is not the sort of thing that even Mr Gladstone would have done for any country except Italy. If he and Lord John had attended a few slave auctions in America we might have heard less about Jeff Davis having "made a nation," and I warrant the *Alabama* would never have sailed.

Gladstone's knowledge of the Italian language and culture was an essential part of his being. Like Milton, he thought of ancient and modern Italy as one, and he was a good deal more interested than Milton in the local Church History. Everything past or present that happened in the peninsula was clothed for him in the light of all sacred and all profane learning. In this spirit he set himself to study Italian history. During the fifties he translated into English Farini's history of the liberal movements in the Papal States under Gregory XVI. and Pio Nono. Tradition has it that, shortly after 1860, when the populace of Naples came to demonstrate in front of his hotel, he addressed them from the balcony, not a little to their astonishment, in a speech of two hours, in Italian, on the need for the new kingdom of Italy to adopt Free Trade. I cannot vouch for the authenticity of the tale, but it is at least in character.

Lord John Russell was less interested in Church History,

but otherwise his feelings about the sacred peninsula were the same as Mr Gladstone's. Lord John, indeed, had never been a Conservative; he had inherited from Fox, Holland and Grey their principles of Liberalism in Continental politics, together with their devotion to Italian literature and to the society of cultivated Italians, of which I spoke above in the case of those statesmen of an earlier age. In the later era, when Lord John flourished, England was sheltering many Italian exiles of the same mental calibre as Ugo Foscolo—men like Panizzi, Poerio, Lacaita, with whom Lord John's family life became closely associated. By the kindness of his daughter, Lady Agatha Russell, I have seen much of his and Lady John Russell's correspondence, from which it is clear that all through the fifties he had been following every turn of Italian politics from inside private information, and living in his own home in an atmosphere of well-informed Italian patriotism. That is why, when he became Foreign Minister, he was able to do the right thing at each stage of the crisis of 1860.

Above all, Lord John believed in Hudson. Hudson was one of those Englishmen of whom there are always a few in every age, who devote their best powers to the unofficial service of some foreign country, track out its most intimate secrets, and understand its true interests and opportunities with an amazing sureness of instinct. Such men are seldom in our diplomatic service. But Hudson was our Minister at Turin in Italy's year. It is probable that he understood the real bearing of Cavour's policy from day to day as well as any man alive. Now the prime fact of our diplomatic success in 1860 is that Hudson carried on a private correspondence with Lord and Lady John Russell behind the back of his own secret official dispatches—a correspondence in which he criticized in the light of every new situation the official policy that he was carrying out at Russell's behest. Thus and thus only was he able to keep British policy moving fast enough to keep pace with the rapidity of events in a year of revolution. He could not have done this with

Russell's Conservative predecessor, nor yet with Palmerston. But he could do it with the Russells, and it saved Italy.

First, he persuaded Lord John to accept the *fait accompli* of the cession of Nice and Savoy to France, as being the necessary payment to Napoleon for permission to liberate any further portions of Italy. Secondly, when Garibaldi had conquered Sicily, Hudson persuaded Lord John, and through him Palmerston, Gladstone, and all England, that the hour had struck for the complete unity of the whole peninsula in one state—a solution to which Palmerston, Gladstone, Russell and Hudson himself had been hitherto opposed, and to which France and the Central Powers continued hostile. To give effect to this change of view, Hudson was just in time, through the agency of Lacaita, to prevent Russell from joining in Napoleon's design to stop Garibaldi at the Straits of Messina. This action to prevent Garibaldi's further progress would have been in accordance with the publicly announced policy of Cavour, but contrary to Cavour's secret wishes, which were known to Hudson. Any action other than that which Russell actually took would have been fatal to. Italian unity; and any minister but Russell, nay, Russell himself with different coaching, would have acted otherwise.

There went so many miracles to make Italy—the miracle men, Mazzini, Garibaldi, Cavour, the right king on the right throne, the thousand wonderful chances of battle and debate—that we sometimes overlook a miracle second to none, that in the year 1860 an English Foreign Minister thoroughly understood, by years of previous study and from the best actual sources of information, the main question with which he was called upon to deal.

# IF NAPOLEON HAD WON THE BATTLE OF WATERLOO[1]

THE day of the signature of the Convention of Brussels, 26th June 1815, is the point of time that divides into two strangely contrasted halves the greatest career of modern times, and ushers in the reign of the Napoleon of Peace. When, in that little room in the Hôtel de Ville, now filled every morning by crowds of tourists, the red-coated patrician, who had once been regarded by his partial countrymen as the rival of the lord of armies, sat listening in proud and stoical humiliation to the torrent of words poured forth in dispraise of war by his perambulatory host, who, with clenched fists, invoked the Goddess of Peace, the laconic Englishman probably thought that he was present at a Napoleonic farce of the usual character. He did not guess that his conqueror had in all truth drained the cup of Peace, a draught as bitter to Napoleon as defeat was bitter to his conquered foe. Wellington, indeed, during the terrible week between the battle and the Convention, had not uttered one complaint against Blücher for breaking tryst, nor shown to his staff officers one sign of his agony— beyond the disuse of his customary oaths.

A new Napoleon had been evolved, the Napoleon of Peace, a mere shadow, in spiritual and intellectual force, of his former self. The Buonaparte of 1796 would have urged the advance of Ney's columns until they had destroyed the last of Wellington's regiments, and would himself, with the bulk of his army, have fallen on the traces of Blücher, instead of suffering him to effect a junction with the Austrians and Russians, and so present a barrier to the French reconquest of Germany. Nor would the Napoleon of 1813, who refused, in defeat, the most favour-

---

[1] In July 1907 the *Westminster Gazette* offered a prize for an essay on this subject. This was the successful essay.

able offers of a settlement, have hesitated after such a victory as that of Mont-Saint-Jean to undertake with a light heart the subjugation of Central and Eastern Europe. But the Napoleon of 1815, one week after his triumphal entry into Brussels, was offering to Wellington the same facilities to evacuate the seat of war which the English general had offered at Cintra, seven years before, to the defeated lieutenant of the Emperor. And this unexpected clemency was extended to England, in order as easily and as quickly as possible to remove from the scene of affairs and from the counsels of the Continental monarchs the paymaster and inveterate instigator of war, and so to clear the stage for Napoleon and the time-serving Metternich to arrange by collusion a permanent and lasting peace for all Europe, not exclusive of England herself.

Whence came this extraordinary change in the intentions, one might say in the character, of the French Emperor? The history of what passed in the headquarters at Brussels between 16th and 26th June can never be fully known, though whole libraries have been written upon the subject. Secret agents of Metternich had been in Brussels as early as 14th June, with orders, in case Wellington were defeated, instantly to offer Napoleon the Rhine frontier and the bulk of the Italian peninsula, and to represent to him how utterly impossible it was that he should hold down Germany after the national movement of 1813. The latter argument, though based upon a just insight into the condition of the Fatherland, would have had little effect upon the man to whom it was addressed had he been sure of support from France herself. But, so far from being dazzled by the news of Mont-Saint-Jean, Paris, on 20th June, formed a determined alliance of all classes and all parties—Liberals, Jacobins, Royalists and old servants of the Empire—to insist upon peace. The representatives commissioned by the Chambers and by other bodies, official and unofficial alike, were welcomed in the Belgian capital, and supported in their petition by all the marshals and by almost every superior officer. But Napoleon's will, it appears, was not finally overcome until the great review of 24th June, held outside the town for the purpose of testing the attitude of the common soldiers. Though most of them were veterans, they had too lately rejoined the camp to be altogether insensible to the national feeling; many of them had come out to liberate France, not to subjugate Europe—a task which no longer seemed as easy as before the days of Borodino and Leipzig. The long shout for "Peace" that ran down the lines seems to have dazed the Emperor. He spoke no word to the assembled troops to thank them for the late victory, rode slowly back like one in a trance, dismounted in the square, passed through the ante-chamber staring vacantly at his marshals and ministers as if on men whom he had never seen before. As he reached the threshold of his Cabinet his eye lit upon the Mameluke by the door, who alone in all the crowd was gazing with intense devotion on his master. The Corsican stopped and, still in a reverie, interpellated the Oriental: "The Franks are tired of war, and we two cannot ride out alone. Besides, we are growing old. One grows old and dies. The Pyramids they grow old, but they do not die." Then, with intense energy, he added: "Do you think one will be remembered after forty centuries?" He stood for a moment, as if waiting for an answer from the mute, then dashed through the door, flung himself at the table, and began dictating messages of peace to Wellington and the Allied Sovereigns.

Napoleon's physical condition probably contributed no less than the attitude of the French army and people to the formation of his great resolution; during the critical week, the decision between peace and war seems to have been as much as he could attend to in his waking hours, which were greatly curtailed by his peculiar malady. Hence it was that he made no serious effort to follow Blücher's retreat through Namur, beyond leaving a free hand to Grouchy. Though he was not yet sufficiently cognizant of his growing feebleness to delegate to anyone either his

military or political duties, he seems to have been sub-
consciously aware that the two together were beyond his
strength. It is, therefore, not strange that he decided to
accept the Rhine frontier and the hegemony in the Italian
peninsula as the basis of a permanent peace, and that his
ever-increasing lassitude of body kept him faithful to the
decision during the last twenty years of his life.

Those years were a period of but slight change for Europe.
Monarchs and peoples were too much exhausted to engage
in war for the alteration of frontiers; internal reform or
revolution was rendered impossible by the great standing
armies, which the very existence of Napoleon on the French
throne, valetudinarian though he was known to be, rendered
necessary, or at least excusable, in England, Austria and
the German states. Hatred of the crowned Jacobin and
fear of renewed French invasions gave to the governments
of the *ancien régime* a measure of popularity with the middle
classes which they would not otherwise have enjoyed; it
has even been suggested that reform might have made
some notable step forward in England within twenty years
of Mont-Saint-Jean had the great Tory champion succeeded
in overthrowing the revolutionary Emperor on the field of
battle.

As it was, the condition of England was most unhappy.
In spite of the restoration of trade with the Continent,
impeded indeed by the extravagantly high tariffs due to
Napoleon's military ideas of economic science, in spite of
our continued supremacy at sea, the distress grew yearly
more intolerable, among both the rural and industrial
populations. The taxation necessary for the maintenance
of both fleet and army on a war footing allowed no hope
of amelioration; yet while Napoleon lived, and paraded his
own army and fleet as the expensive toys of his old age,
the Tory Ministers could see no possibility of reduction
on their part. Probably they were glad of the excuse, for
the great army enabled them to defy the Reformers, who
became ever more violent as year after year passed by

without prospect of change. If Mont-Saint-Jean had been a victory for England, and if it had been followed by that general disarmament to which Wellington himself had looked forward as the natural consequence of Napoleon's downfall, Catholic Emancipation must have been granted to Ireland, and this concession would at least have averted the constant revolts and massacres in that unhappy country which so sorely tempted Napoleon to resume hostilities during the last ten years of his life. In Great Britain, where starvation and repression were the order of the day, there occurred in 1825 the ill-advised but romantic rebellion of Lord Byron, in whose army the rank and file consisted almost entirely of working men, and the leaders (except Napier) had no more knowledge of war than was possessed by such ruffians as Thistlewood and the ex-pirate Trelawny. The savage reprisals of Government established the blood-feud between one half of England and the other. Byron's execution made a greater noise in the world than any event since the fall of the Bastille, though it was not immediately followed by political changes. After two years of terror, Canning, who was always suspected by his colleagues of semi-popular sympathies, restored partial freedom of the Press in 1827, and it became apparent in the literature of the next decade that all young men of spirit were no longer Anti-Jacobins—no longer even Whigs, but Radicals. The worship of the dead poet went side by side with the worship of the living. The writings of Shelley, especially after his long imprisonment, obtained a popularity which was one of the most curious symptoms of the time. His *Men of England, wherefore plough?* was sung at all Radical gatherings, and his ode on the death of Napoleon (*The Dead Anarch*, 1836) passed through twenty-five editions in a year. The younger literary stars, like Tennyson and Arthur Hallam, blazed with revolutionary ardour. Excluded from Oxford and Cambridge, the Dissenters and Radicals formed a university at Manchester, which soon almost monopolized the talent of the country. Meanwhile, serious politicians like Lord

John Russell and the irrepressible Mr Brougham abandoned the older Whig creed and declared for Universal Suffrage. No wise man, in the year after Napoleon's death, would have foretold with confidence whether England was destined to tread the path of revolution or to continue in the beaten track of tyranny and obscurantism. At least it was clear that there was no longer any third way open to her, and that the coming era would be stained with blood and violence. Whiggery died with Grey—that pathetic and futile figure, who had waited forty years in vain. The English character was no longer one of compromise; it was being forced by foreign circumstances into another and more violent mould.

Similarly in the Continental states, outside the limits of the Napoleonic Empire, the *ancien régime* was not only triumphant but to some extent popular and national, because the late persecutor of the German and Spanish peoples still remained as their dangerous neighbour, and was still by far the most powerful prince in Europe. In Spain the liberals and free-thinkers were extirpated with an efficiency which Torquemada might have approved; the Inquisition was indeed abolished in consequence of Napoleon's threat of war in 1833—a year in which the Tories were unable to give Spain diplomatic support, because the execution of the eccentric " gypsy-Englishman " for smuggling Bibles into Andalusia had raised a momentary storm among their evangelical supporters in the House and country. But the disappearance of the Inquisition made no real difference to the methods of Church and State in Spain, and the diplomatic incident only served, as it was intended, to restore the old Emperor's popularity with the French liberals.

Meanwhile the revolted Spanish colonies in South America continued their efforts for freedom with ever-increasing success until the interference of the English army, sent out by Government on pure Anti-Jacobin principles, against the wish and the interest of the British merchants trading in those parts. " We must preserve," said Castle-reagh, " the balance between Monarchy and Republicanism in the New World as in the Old." But not enough troops could be spared from policing the British Islands to do more than prolong the agony of the transatlantic struggle. The vast expanses of the Pampas became a permanent Field of Mars, where liberal exiles and adventurers of all countries, principally English and Italian, side by side with the well-mounted Gauchos, waged a ceaseless guerrilla war on the English and Spanish regulars. Here Napier's brothers avenged his death on the army of which they had once been the ornaments; and Murat, riding-whip in hand, was seen at the head of many a gallant charge, leading on the Italians whose idol he had now become in either hemisphere. " The free life of the Pampas" became to the young men of Europe the symbol of that spiritual and political emancipation which could be realized only in exile and secured in rebellion and in war. Hence it is that the note of the Pampas is as prevalent as the note of Byron in the literature and art of that epoch.

In Germany the national hopes of union and liberty were cheated by the monarchs, who continued, however, to enjoy safety, prestige and the bodyguard of those great standing armies which were necessary to secure French respect for the Rhine frontier. The reforms previously effected in those German states which had been either subject to Napoleon's rule or moved by his example, were permitted to remain, wherever they made for the strength of the monarchic principle. The Prussian peasants were not thrust back into serfdom; the reformed Civil Service was kept in some of the " Westphalian " states; the Act of Mediation and the Abolition of the Prince-Bishoprics were maintained for the benefit of the larger princes. But all traces of the *Code Napoléon* were abolished in Hesse-Cassel and Hanover; while the University and National movements were effectively suppressed throughout the Fatherland under Austrian influence, paramount since the failure of Blücher in Flanders and the deal between Metternich and Napoleon at the Conference of Vienna in 1815. If Prussia obtained nothing else, she recovered her share of Poland, whose cries were smothered by the Christian Powers of the East as easily as Greece was put down by the Turk.

The only Germans who were at once contented and well governed were those on the left bank of the Rhine, who continued to be, in peace as in war, the quietest and most loyal of all Napoleon's subjects. The French were less easy to satisfy; they had, indeed, forced their lord to make peace, but could they also compel him to grant that measure of liberty which they now claimed? The solution of that question would scarcely have been possible except by violent means had the Emperor retained half of his old health and vigour. But it was solved provisionally from year to year, because the energies of the autocrat decreased in almost exact proportion to the increase of his subjects' demand for freedom. He cared not who wielded powers which he was no longer in a condition to exercise himself, and was ready, out of sheer indifference, to hand them scornfully over to ministers more or less in sympathy with the Chambers. So long as he could keep his own eye on the censorship it was rigid; but when he became too ill to read anything except the most important dispatches the censorship was again as feebly administered as in the days of the last two Bourbons. Under these conditions of irritating but ineffectual repression, French literature and thought were stimulated into a life almost as flourishing as in the days of the Encyclopædists. The Romantic movement undermined the Imperial idea with the intellectuals; the "breath of the Pampas" was felt in the Quartier Latin. It was in vain that the police broke the busts of Byron and forbade plays in which the unities were violated.

Yet as long as Napoleon lived, and let live the liberals, the quarrel of the ruled against their ruler was but half serious. The movement towards a fresh revolution was rather a preparation for his death than a very deliberate disloyalty to the man who had saved France from the *ancien régime*. And, whatever the workmen and students might think, the peasants and soldiers regarded the political and social condition of France after Mont Saint-Jean as almost perfect. The soldiers were still the favourites of Government; the peasants at length tilled in peace and security the lands which their fathers had seized from the nobles and the clergy. The religion of the vast majority of Frenchmen was respected, but the priest was confined to the Church; the home and the women belonged to the father of the family, and the school to the State.

Indeed, the chief cause of complaint against Napoleon's government, in the eyes of the majority of his subjects, was not political, social or religious, but administrative. The executive machine at Paris, to which the life of the remotest hamlets was "mortised and adjoined," worked with an inefficiency resultant on the bad health of the autocrat. His personal attention to business became more and more irregular, and, since the ineradicable tradition of the Imperial service was to wait upon his initiative, France was scarcely better governed from the Tuileries in 1820 than she had been in 1807 from the camp-fires of Poland.

In the treaties of autumn 1815 the wily Metternich had succeeded, by a masterpiece of cunning, in retaining the Venetian territories for Austria as the price of abandoning at the conference the claims of Prussia to expansion in Germany. As in Northern Europe the Rhine, so in Italy the Mincio, became the geographic boundary between the Napoleonic system and the *ancien régime*—both as yet rather feebly threatened by the rising spirit of Italian nationality. Murat, who had by his recent conduct fairly sacrificed the goodwill of both parties, lost his kingdom and fled to South America. No one dared to propose to Napoleon the restoration of the temporal power of the Pope; it had, indeed, no more claim to recognition than that of the prince-bishops, whose recently secularized territories none of the German princes proposed to restore. Sicily, protected by the British ships, remained to the House of Bourbon. From the moment that the signature of peace removed the fear of the French invasion British influence waned at Palermo, and the old methods of Sicilian despotism returned. But the fact that the King of Sicily was obliged by the Powers to renounce all his claims to the throne of Naples stood him in good stead with his insular subjects, whose jealousy was appeased by this act of separation.

All the Italian peninsula, except the territory of Venice, was subject to the unifying influence of the French Imperial system. The *Code Napoléon*, the encouragement of the middle class, the abeyance of clerical influence in government and education in favour of military and official ideals, continued as before the peace. The clerical and liberal forces, still divided by the deadliest enmity, which would certainly break out in bloodshed if the foreigner were ever to be expelled from Italy, were alike hostile to the French. But whereas the clericals hoped to restore the *ancien régime*, either by extending the Austrian dominions or calling back the native princes, and especially the Pope, the liberals, on the other hand, dreamed of an Italian Republic. These two movements were represented to Italy and to the world—the one by the Prince of the House of Savoy, the hope of the reactionaries, and the other by the son of the Genoese doctor, the founder of the formidable " Società Savonarola," in which many of the rising generation hastened to enlist themselves. In 1832 both these romantic young men fell victims to Napoleon's police; Charles Albert was detected in disguise in Turin, and suffered the fate of the Duc d'Enghien. Mazzini, who had the year before escaped with difficulty from the Venetian Alps, where he had raised the national flag against Austria, attempted a rising against Napoleon in the streets of Genoa, but being opposed by the Italian soldiery, who found all that they wanted in the existing regime, was captured and shot, with twelve of his followers.

# IF NAPOLEON HAD WON

The executions of the Savoyard prince and the Genoese prophet served to remind Europe that Napoleon, in his old age, still remained, as in his youth, the enemy alike of the *ancien régime* and of democratic liberty. Which of the two would be the chief gainer by his death it was impossible to predict.

On the evening of 4th June 1836, Napoleon was presiding, with even more than his habitual invalid's lethargy, at one of his Councils of State. The latest reports from Italy were presented, and a closer *entente* with the Austrian police was under discussion. The Emperor had been sitting, silent and distracted, his head sunk on his breast. Suddenly the word "Italy" penetrated to his consciousness. He looked up with fire in his eyes. "Italy!" he said; "we march to-morrow. The army of the Alps will deserve well of the Republic." Then, more distractedly, he murmured: "I must leave Joséphine behind. She will not care." He had often of late been talking thus of his first Empress, whom he seemed to imagine to be somewhere in the palace, but unwilling to see him. It was the custom of the Council, dictated by the physicians, to adjourn as soon as he mentioned her name. The Ministers therefore retired.

The rest of the story can best be told by M. Villebois, physician of the Imperial Household:

"While the Council sat I was walking in the Tuileries Gardens below. It was a hot and silent night of June. The city was at rest and the trees slept with her. Suddenly, from the open window of the Council Chamber, a noise, inconceivably unmelodious, makes itself heard. I look up, and behold the Emperor standing alone at the balcony, with the lights behind him framing him like a picture. With the gestures of a wild animal just set free, he is intoning, in a voice of the most penetrating discord, the Revolutionary hymn of France, which he has forbidden under penalty of the law to the use of his subjects. But to him, I know it, it is not a hymn of revolution but a *chant*

134

*du départ.* I rush upstairs, and find a group of Ministers and lackeys trembling outside the door. No one dares enter. 'Doctor,' said old Marshal ——, 'he sang that cursed song like that the night before we crossed into Russia. On that occasion we stood in the room below and trembled, and one told me that he had sung it thus, in solitude, on the night before he first crossed into Italy.'

" Pushing past the brave old man, I opened the door and entered alone. The sound had now ceased, but the song had penetrated through the summer night, and in the Rue de Rivoli a drunken *ouvrier* had caught it up and was thundering it out. I looked round for my master, and did not at first see him. Suddenly I perceived that Napoleon was lying dead at my feet. I heard the oaths of the *ouvrier* as the police seized him under the arcade."

# THE NEWS OF RAMILLIES

## A CAMBRIDGE FANTASY [1]

[*Pages from the Cambridge diary of Tom Slippers, Sizar of Trinity College, and afterwards for thirty years Curate to the Vicar of Bray Parish.*]

*May* 27, 1706. Scarce in time at the College Chapel this morning, and thought I saw the Dean frown upon me as I went past him. The Master [2] was at the service, which made us all wonder, until coming out into the Court I found many outside the door, and the Master telling them how he had received news at midnight, from an outrider of my Lord Godolphin, that a glorious victory had been won by my Lord the Duke of Marlboro' over the Marshal Villeroi in the Low Countries. [3] Whereat I to breakfast very glad of heart, and Smithers must needs have up into our garret two pints ale to drink my Lord Duke his health before we fell to our books; nor would he be gainsaid, though it is my custom to drink water at breakfast, as my careful father directed me. There are some of the wealthier sort do now drink coffee o' mornings, which liquor my tutor holds to be the famous black broth of the Spartans. (Mem. query?)

We went forth at noon to disport ourselves at walking. Smithers would have played football in the backsides, but I showed him that it was but a lewd game and that in my father's time none played it save those who were of St John the Evangelist's (*vulgo* Porci); on hearing which he was well satisfied to walk only. We two going forth, saw standing upon the bridge that very Whig the Earl of Kingsdown Charteris. Whereat I made to turn back,

---

[1] Reprinted from the *Cambridge Review*, May Week Number, 1901.
[2] Bentley (ed. of MS.).
[3] Ramillies.

thinking to go round by Clare, for whenever his lordship meets me, he is pleased to be very merry (*exempli gratiâ,* asking whether the cobbler doth not pinch my feet), as he will do to all us poor parsons' sons. But now, as I was turning, he called to me, taking off his hat mannerly and said, " Mr Slippers, I trust that you're for the honest party and ' Goddam-the-French-King.' " [1] Whereat being much pleased, "Yes, my lord," scarce knowing what I said. " Then," saith he, " I will send for you this evening to help us hold the court to-night and shout for her Majesty's Ministers."

When we had passed out of hearing of his lordship up the new avenue towards Coton, Smithers saith to me, " What's this, Tom, art turned ranter? I thought you were for Church and State." [2] At that I turned to him and spoke, as I conceive, with some spirit. " So I am," I said, " and for Goddam-the-French-King too." (Mem. and query—Is it a fault thus to use an oath in a catch-word? Shall ask my tutor.) "A plague on your parties," say I, " that an honest fellow cannot go about his business, no, nor so much as get his curacy, without this party give it to him and that party try to take it from him."

Went round over Madingley Hill and viewed that fair seat of Sir John Cotton, Bart. Coming back through the town we saw a gazette from London, just arrived, all hot. Smithers in much concern for his cousin Frank, an officer among the hand-grenade men, of whom he is very proud. The gazette tells how the regiment before which his company marches was set to storm the village, but no list of the slain yet. All the Kingsmen walking in the streets in high glee, they esteeming themselves to be of the Duke's kin, because forsooth his son was at their College, which I think a very poor conceit. (Query—why are Kingsmen so proud?) Towards nightfall I bolted the door of our room, fearing

[1] In 1706 Marlborough, Godolphin and the Whigs were carrying on the war against Louis XIV.; the High Tories were lukewarm in their support of it.
[2] That is, High Church and Tory.

the young Whigs would come to take me with them. And to be sure one did soon call from below, and then what a rushing of feet up to the garret, and a kicking against the panels. Whereat I, fearing harm to the door, and that making forced entry they might put some notable slight upon the print of King Charles the Martyr that my father gave me, was fain to go out and down with them into the court, where was all the youth of the College except the stricter sort of Tories. Whenever one of that party showed himself at the foot of his staircase, even if he was but passing to another's rooms, he was driven in with cries, at peril of his person. The Earl of Kingsdown Charteris took a hold of Lord Jacobus Towrow, and was for putting him into the great conduit, hap-splash and under; but no one else dared touch a lord in this manner.

It being now about nine o'clock, the Earl had tables and Portuguese wine [1] set in the court, and all who passed must needs drink Whig toasts. I now began to be very merry, and marched gladly round and round the court. Now and again we would stop under the windows of some notable of the other side and give three cheers for the Duke or the Lord Treasurer, till the one above poured out water, if he held his door to be strong. But we never cheered for the Queen, but only for her servants, which was much remarked on.

We stopped under Sir Isaac Newton's rooms, between the gate and the chapel, and gave three cheers for the philosopher, who is of the Whig party; howsoever he looked not forth. After that the Earl of Kingsdown would have us stop before the Lodge and give three cheers for that good Whig, Dr Bentley, yet methought it was but a weak shout. (Mem.—Here I shouted not, knowing the doctor to be but a poor scholar, as my tutor has often told me; *exempli gratiâ* his denial of Phalaris his letters.) The Master, indeed, sending out to know what the matter was, when

---

[1] Port was the drink favoured by the Whigs and the war party, in preference to that strong argument for peace—French claret.

he heard it to be a Whig mob that cheered for the victory, let the matter be, which was very ill thought of by the seniors.

We now, being very merry, began to march round trampling like a battalia, and singing the new song made for the army of " The British Grenadiers," where their martial deeds are extolled above those of Greek Hercules or Roman Cæsar. In the chorus the skill ever is to make a noise like a drum beating (tow, row, row), which we did but indifferently well till one fetched a drum, whereat we took to singing the chorus again and again, and cheering for my Lord the Duke of Marlboro'. Then some one began to sing a ribald song, of which the chorus was:

" We'll scent them out whene'er we can,
The Pope, the Devil, and the Warming Pan,"

which I take to be in very deed the policy of that Party. Some did rumour that the song was first written to divert that horrible and wicked spawn of Satan the C-lv-s H--d Cl-b, founded, as men say, by the regicide John Milton. (O Christ's College, what a monster didst thou bring forth! thou shalt be equal in infamy to Sidney Sussex, the cradle of the Divil Noll himself!) Howsoever, the song was a merry song, and though it were scarce honest to set more of it down, I have it in my head.

Coming back to my rooms found Smithers very sour, who for conscience sake had not gone down into the court. " Thou apparent anabaptist! " quoth he. " Thou patent nonjuror and concealed papist! " quo' I.

*May* 28. Late for Chapel this morning.

# CLIO, A MUSE [1]

THE last fifty years have witnessed great changes in the management of Clio's temple. Her inspired prophets and bards have passed away and been succeeded by the priests of an established church; the vulgar have been excluded from the Court of the Gentiles; doctrine has been defined; heretics have been excommunicated; and the tombs of the aforesaid prophets have been duly blackened by the new hierarchy. While these changes were in process the statue of the Muse was seen to wink an eye. Was it in approval, or in derision?

Two generations back, history was a part of our national literature, written by persons moving at large in the world of letters or politics. Among them were a few writers of genius, and many of remarkable talent, who did much to mould the thought and inspire the feeling of the day.

Of recent years the popular influence of history has greatly diminished. The thought and feeling of the rising generation is but little affected by historians. History was, by her own friends, proclaimed a "science" for specialists, not "literature" for the common reader of books. And the common reader of books has accepted his discharge.

That is one half of the revolution. But, fortunately, that is not all. Whereas fifty years ago history had no standing in higher education, and even twenty years ago but little, to-day Clio is driving the classical Athene out of the field, as the popular arts course in our universities. The good results attained by university historical teaching, when brought to bear on the raw product of our public schools, is a great fact in modern education. But it means very hard work for the history dons, who, in the time they can spare from these heavy educational tasks, must write the modern

[1] First published in this form in 1913; somewhat altered from an article in the *Independent Review*, 1904.

history-books. Fifty years ago there were no such people; to-day they are a most important but sadly overworked class of men.

Such is the double aspect of the change in the status of history. The gain in the deeper academic life of the nation must be set off against the loss in its wider literary life. To ignore either is to be most partial. But must we always submit to the loss in order to secure the gain? Already during the last decade there are signs in the highest quarters of a reconciling process, of a synthesis of the scientific to the literary view of history. Streaks of whitewash have been observed on the tombs of those bards and prophets whose bones Professor Seeley burned. When no less an authority than Professor Firth thinks it worth while to edit Macaulay; when Mr Gooch in his *History of Historians* can give an admirable appreciation of Carlyle, times are evidently changing a little in those high places whence ideas gradually filter down through educational England. Isis and Camus, reverend sires, foot it slow—but sure. It is then in no cantankerous spirit against the present generation of academic historians, but in all gratitude, admiration and personal friendship towards them, that I launch this "delicate investigation" into the character of history. What did the Muse mean when she winked?

These new History Schools, still at the formative period of their growth, are to the world of older learning what Western Canada is to England to-day. Settlers pour into the historical land of promise who, a generation back, would have striven for a livelihood in the older "schools" and "triposes." The danger to new countries with a population rapidly increasing is lest life there grow up hastily into a raw materialism, a dead level of uniform ambition all directed to the mere acquisition of dollars. In the historical world the analogue of the almighty dollar is the crude document. If a student digs up a new documen he is happy, he has succeeded; if not he is unhappy, h has failed. There is some danger that the overwhelming rush of immigrants into the new History Schools may cause us to lose some of the old culture and the great memories. But I hope that we shall not be forgetful of the mother country.

And who is the mother country to Anglo-Saxon historians? Some reply "Germany," but others of us prefer to answer "England." The methods and limitations of German learning presumably suit the Germans, but are certain to prove a strait-waistcoat to English limbs and faculties. We ought to look to the free, popular literary traditions of history in our own land. Until quite recent times, from the days of Clarendon down through Gibbon, Carlyle and Macaulay to Green and Lecky, historical writing was not merely the mutual conversation of scholars with one another, but was the means of spreading far and wide throughout all the reading classes a love and knowledge of history, an elevated and critical patriotism, and certain qualities of mind and heart. But all that has been stopped, and an attempt has been made to drill us into so many Potsdam Guards of learning.

We cannot, however, decide this question on a mere point of patriotism. It is necessary to ask *a priori* whether the modern German or the old English ideal was the right one. It is necessary to ask, "What is history and what is its use?" We must "gang ower the fundamentals," as the old Scottish lady with the ear-trumpet said so alarmingly to the new minister when he entered her room on his introductory visit. So I now ask, what is the object of the life of man *quâ* historian? Is it to know the past and enjoy it for ever? Or is it to do one's duty to one's neighbour and cause him also to know the past? The answer to these theoretic questions must have practical effects on the teaching and learning, the writing and reading of history.

The root questions can be put in these terms: "Ought history to be merely the accumulation of facts about the past? Or ought it also to be the interpretation of facts about the past? Or, one step farther, ought it to be not merely the accumulation and interpretation of facts, but also the exposition of these facts and opinions *in their full emotional and intellectual value* to a wide public by the difficult art of literature? "

The words in italics raise another question which can be put thus:

" Ought emotion to be excluded from history on the ground that history deals only with the science of cause and effect in human affairs? "

It will be well to begin the discussion by considering the alleged " science of cause and effect in human affairs." This alleged " science " does not exist, and cannot ever exist in any degree of accuracy remotely deserving to be described by the word " science." The idea that the facts of history are of value as part of an exact science confined to specialists is due to a misapplication of the analogy of physical science. Physical science would still be of immense, though doubt-less diminished, value even if the general public had no smattering thereof, even if Sir Robert Ball had never lectured, and Huxley had never slaughtered bishops for a Roman holiday.

The functions of physical science are mainly two: direct utility in practical fields; and in more intellectual fields the deduction of laws of " cause and effect." Now history can perform neither of these functions.

In the first place it has no practical utility like physical science. No one can by a knowledge of history, however profound, invent the steam-engine, or light a town, or cure cancer, or make wheat grow near the Arctic Circle. For this reason there is not in the case of history, as there is in the case of physical science, any utilitarian value at all in the accumulation of knowledge by a small number of students, repositories of secrets unknown to the vulgar.

In the second place history cannot, like physical science, deduce causal laws of general application. All attempts have failed to discover laws of "cause and effect" which are certain to repeat themselves in the institutions and affairs of men. The law of gravitation may be scientifically proved because it is universal and simple. But the historical law that starvation brings on revolt is not proved; indeed the opposite statement, that starvation leads to abject submission, is equally true in the light of past events. You cannot so completely isolate any historical event from its circumstances as to be able to deduce from it a law of general application. Only politicians adorning their speeches with historical arguments have this power; and even they never agree. An historical event cannot be isolated from its circumstances any more than the onion from its skins, because an event is itself nothing but a set of circumstances, none of which will ever recur.

To bring the matter to the test, what are the "laws" which historical "science" has discovered in the last forty years, since it cleared the laboratory of those wretched "literary historians"? Medea has successfully put the old man into the pot, but I fail to see the fine youth whom she promised us.

Not only can no causal laws of universal application be discovered in so complex a subject, but the interpretation of the cause and effect of any one particular event cannot rightly be called "scientific." The collection of facts, the weighing of evidence as to what events happened, are in some sense scientific; but not so the discovery of the causes and effects of those events. In dealing even with an affair of which the facts are so comparatively well known as those of the French Revolution, it is impossible accurately to examine the psychology of twenty-five million different persons, of whom—except a few hundreds or thousands—the lives and motives are buried in the black night of the utterly forgotten. No one, therefore, can ever give a complete or wholly true account of the causes of the French Revolution. But several imperfect readings of history are better than none at all; and he will give the best interpretation who, having discovered and weighed all the important evidence obtainable, has the largest grasp of intellect, the warmest human sympathy, the highest imaginative powers.

Carlyle, at least in his greatest work, fulfilled the last two conditions, and therefore his psychology of the mob in the days of mob rule, his flame-picture of what was in very fact a conflagration, his portraits of individual characters—Louis, Sieyès, Danton, Marat, Robespierre — are in the most important sense more true than the cold analysis of the same events and the conventional summings up of the same persons by scientific historians who, with more knowledge of facts, have less understanding of Man. It was not till later in his life that Carlyle went mad with hero-worship and ceased to understand his fellow-men with that all-embracing tolerance and sympathy which is the spiritual hall-mark of his *French Revolution*.

The weakness of that great book is that its author knew nothing in detail about the *ancien régime* and the "Old French Form of Life" that was destroyed. He described the course of the fire, but he knew nothing of the combustibles or of the match.

How, indeed, could history be a "science"? You can dissect the body of a man, and argue thence the general structure of the bodies of other men. But you cannot dissect a mind; and if you could, you could not argue thence about other minds. You can know nothing scientifically of the twenty million minds of a nation. The few facts we know may or may not be typical of the rest. Therefore, in the most important part of its business, history is not a scientific deduction, but an imaginative guess at the most likely generalizations.

History is only in part a matter of "fact." Collect the "facts" of the French Revolution! You must go down to hell and up to heaven to fetch them. The pride of the physical scientist is attacked, and often justly. But what is his pride compared with the pride of the historian who thinks that his collection of " facts " will suffice for a scientific study of cause and effect in human affairs?

" The economist," said Professor Marshall,[1] " needs imagination above all to put him on the track of those causes of events which are remote or lie below the surface." Now if, as Professor Marshall tells us, imagination is necessary for the economist, by how much more is it necessary for the historian, if he wishes to discover the causes of man's action, not merely as a bread-winning individual, but in all his myriad capacities of passion and of thought! The man who is himself devoid of emotion or enthusiasm can seldom credit, and can never understand, the emotions of others, which have none the less played a principal part in cause and effect. Therefore, even if history were a science of cause and effect, that would be a reason not for excluding but for including emotion as part of the historian's method.

It was no unemotional historian, but the author of *Sartor Resartus*, who found out that Cromwell was not a hypocrite. Carlyle did not arrive at this result by a strictly deductive process, but it was none the less true, and, unlike many historical discoveries, it was of great value. Carlyle, indeed, sometimes neglected the accumulation of facts and the proper sifting of evidence. He is not to be imitated as a model historian, but he should be read and considered by all historical students, because of his imaginative and narrative qualities. While he lacks what modern historical method has acquired, he possesses in the fullest degree what it has lost.

Carlyle uses constantly an historical method which Gibbon and Maitland use sometimes, and other historians scarcely at all—humour. The " dignity of history," whether literary or scientific, is too often afraid of contact with the comic spirit. Yet there are historical situations, just as there are domestic and social situations, which can be treated usefully or even truthfully only by seeing the fun of them. How

[1] *Economic Teaching at the Universities in Relation to Public Well-Being.*

else could Anacharsis Clootz' Deputation of the Human Species to the French Assembly be profitably told? "From bench and gallery comes 'repeated applause'; for what august Senator but is flattered even by the very shadow of the Human Species depending on him? Anacharsis and the 'Foreigners' Committee' shall have place at the Federation; on condition of telling their respective Peoples what they see there. In the meantime, we invite them to the 'honours of the sitting, *honneur de la séance*.' A long-flowing Turk, for rejoinder, bows with Eastern solemnity, and utters articulate sounds; but owing to his imperfect knowledge of the French dialect, his words are like spilt water; the thought he had in him remains conjectural to this day."

I conclude, therefore, that the analogy of physical science has misled many historians during the last thirty years right away from the truth about their profession. There is no utilitarian value in knowledge of the past, and there is no way of scientifically deducing causal laws about the action of human beings in the mass. In short, the value of history is not scientific. Its true value is educational. It can educate the minds of men by causing them to reflect on the past.

Even if cause and effect could be discovered with accuracy, they still would not be the most interesting part of human affairs. It is not man's evolution but his attainment that is the great lesson of the past and the highest theme of history. The deeds themselves are more interesting than their causes and effects, and are fortunately ascertainable with much greater precision. "Scientific" treatment of the evidence (there only can we speak to some extent of "science") can establish with reasonable certainty that such and such events occurred, that one man did this and another said that. And the story of great events is itself of the highest value when it is properly treated by the intellect and the imagination of the historian. The feelings, speculations and actions of the soldiers of Cromwell's army are interesting in themselves, not merely as part of a process of " cause and effect." Doubtless, through the long succeeding centuries the deeds of these men had their effect, as one amid the thousand confused waves that give the impulse to the world's ebb and flow. But how great or small their effect was must be a matter of wide speculation; and the ultimate success or failure, whatever that may have been, was largely ruled by incalculable chance. It is the business of the historian to generalize and to guess as to cause and effect, but he should do it modestly and not call it " science," and he should not regard it as his first duty, which is to tell the story. For, irrespective of " cause and effect," we want to know the thoughts and deeds of Cromwell's soldiers, as one of the higher products and achievements of the human race, a thing never to be repeated, that once took shape and was. And so, too, with Charles and his Cavaliers, we want to know what they were like and what they did, for neither will they ever come again. On the whole, we have been faithfully served in this matter by Carlyle, Gardiner and Professor Firth.

It is the tale of the thing done, even more than its causes and effects, which trains the political judgment by widening the range of sympathy and deepening the approval and disapproval of conscience; that stimulates by example youth to aspire and age to endure; that enables us, by the light of what men once have been, to see the thing we are, and dimly to descry the form of what we should be. " Is not Man's history and Men's history a perpetual evangel? "

It is because the historians of to-day were trained by the Germanizing hierarchy to regard history not as an " evangel " or even as a " story," but as a " science," that they have so much neglected what is after all the principal craft of the historian—the art of narrative. It is in narrative that modern historical writing is weakest, and to my thinking it is a very serious weakness—spinal, in fact. Some writers would seem never to have studied the art of telling a story. There is no " flow " in their events, which

# CLIO, A MUSE

stand like ponds instead of running like streams. Yet history is, in its unchangeable essence, " a tale." Round the story, as flesh and blood round the bone, should be gathered many different things—character-drawing, study of social and intellectual movements, speculations as to probable causes and effects, and whatever else the historian can bring to illuminate the past. But the art of history remains always the art of narrative. That is the bed-rock.

It is possible that, in the days of Carlyle and Macaulay, Motley and Michelet, too much thought was given to narrative, at least in comparison with other aspects of history, for absolutely too much can never be given. It is possible that when Professor Seeley said, " Break the drowsy spell of narrative. Ask yourself questions, set yourself problems," he may have been serving his generation. But it is time now for a swing of the pendulum. " The drowsy spell of narrative " has been broken with a vengeance. Readers find little "spell" in historical narrative nowadays—however it may be with the " drowsiness."

One day, as I was walking along the side of Great Gable, thinking of history and forgetting the mountains which I trod, I chanced to look up and see the top of a long green ridge outlined on the blue horizon. For half-a-minute I stood in thoughtless enjoyment of this new range, noting upon it forms of beauty and qualities of romance, until suddenly I remembered that I was looking at the top of Helvellyn! Instantly, as by magic, its shape seemed to change under my eyes, and the qualities with which I had endowed the unknown mountain to fall away, because I now knew what like were its hidden base and its averted side, what names and memories clung round it. The change taking place in its aspect seemed physical, but I suppose it was only a trick of my own mind. Even so, if we could forget for a while all that had happened since the battle of Waterloo we should see it, not as we see it now, with all its time-honoured associations and its conventionalized place

149

in history, but as our ancestors saw it first, when they did not know whether the "Hundred Days," as we now call them, would not stretch out for a hundred years. Every true history must, by its human and vital presentation of events, force us to remember that the past was once real as the present and uncertain as the future.

Even in our personal experience we have probably noticed the uncanny difference between events when they first appear red-hot, and the same events calmly reviewed, cold and dead, in the perspective of subsequent happenings. I sometimes remember, each time with a shock of surprise, how the Boer War, and the Election of 1906, appeared to me while they were still portents, unsettling our former modes of thought and expectation. Normally I cannot recollect what I then felt. It comes back to me only at chance moments when my mind has let slip all forms and pressures stamped on it in later days. It is not that my worthless "opinions" have altered since then. I am speaking of something much more subtle and potent than "opinions"; I mean the pangs felt by the soul as she hastily adapts herself to new circumstances, when some strange joy or terror, with face half-hid, ineluctably advances. I have forgotten most of it, but I remember some of it sometimes, as in a dream.

Now, if so great a change of emotional attitude towards an event can take place in the same person within a few years, how very different must our view of the battle of Waterloo and of the Reform Bill of 1832 be from the aspect which first they bore to our grandfathers and great-grandfathers, men so very different from ourselves, brought up in habits of thought and conduct long passed away. Deeply are they buried from our sight

> " Under the downtrodden pall
> Of the leaves of many years,"

and sometimes deeper still under the formulæ of conventional history.

# CLIO, A MUSE

To recover some of our ancestors' real thoughts and feelings is the hardest, subtlest and most educative function that the historian can perform. It is much more difficult than to spin guesswork generalizations, the reflex of passing phases of thought or opinion in our own day. To give a true picture of any country, or man or group of men, in the past requires industry and knowledge, for only the documents can tell us the truth, but it requires also insight, sympathy and imagination of the finest, and, last but not least, the art of making our ancestors live again in modern narrative. Carlyle, at his rare best, could do it. If you would know what the night before a *journée* in the French Revolution was like, read his account of the eve of 10th August, in the chapter called "The Steeples at Midnight." Whether or not it is entirely accurate in detail, it is true in effect: the spirit of that long-dead hour rises on us from the night of Time Past. Maitland, too, has done it for the legal side of the English mediæval mind—the only side thereof yet clearly revealed to us except what we see through Chaucer's magic little window.

On a somewhat lower imaginative plane Professor Pollard is doing wonders in showing us how the folks in Tudor times thought about their affairs, political and religious. This is great news, for hitherto the English Reformation has mainly been told from the point of view either of priests, curates or Orangemen of the nineteenth century. Professor Pollard's work is a credit to latter-day history, and is much more true than that of Froude or his opponents. But, although Professor Pollard is one of the most popular living historians, he does not arouse the same amount of public interest that those antagonists used to excite. This is partly, no doubt, because the modern public is less interested in religious controversy. But it is also partly because the modern public is less interested in history, and, by a habit of mind now inbred, thinks that a professional historian must be writing his best books not for the nation but for his fellow-students. And the worst of it is that this lamentable error was put about in the last generation by the historians themselves, when they denounced from the altar any of their profession, alive or dead, who had had dealings with literature.

But since history has no properly scientific value, its only purpose is educative. And if historians neglect to educate the public, if they fail to interest it intelligently in the past, then all their historical learning is valueless except in so far as it educates themselves.

What, then, are the various ways in which history can educate the mind?

The first—or at least the most generally acknowledged —educational effect of history is to train the mind of the citizen into a state in which he is capable of taking a just view of political problems. But, even in this capacity, history cannot prophesy the future; it cannot supply a set of invariably applicable laws for the guidance of politicians; it cannot show, by the deductions of historical analogy, which side is in the right in any quarrel of our own day. It can do a thing less, and yet greater, than all these. It can mould the mind itself into the capability of understanding great affairs and sympathizing with other men. The information given by history is valueless in itself, unless it produce a new state of mind. The value of Lecky's Irish history did not consist in the fact that he recorded in a book the details of numerous massacres and murders, but that he produced sympathy and shame, and caused a better understanding among us all of how the sins of the fathers are often visited upon the children, unto the third and fourth generations of them that hate each other. He does not prove that Home Rule is right or wrong, but he trains the mind of Unionists and Home Rulers to think sensibly about that and other problems.

For it is in this political function of history that the study of cause and effect is of some real use. Though such a study can be neither scientific nor exact, common sense sometimes points to an obvious causal connection. Thus it was supposed, even before the invention of scientific history, that Alva's policy was in some causal connection with the revolt of the Netherlands, that Brunswick's manifesto had something to do with the September Massacres, and the September Massacres with the spread of reaction. Such suggestions of cause and effect in the past help to teach political wisdom. When a man of the world reads history he is called on to form a judgment on a social or political problem, without previous bias, and with some knowledge of the final protracted result of what was done. The exercise of his mind under such unwonted conditions sends him back to the still unsettled problems of modern politics and society, with larger views, clearer head and better temper. The study of past controversies, of which the final outcome is known, destroys the spirit of prejudice. It brings home to the mind the evils that are likely to spring from violent policy, based on want of understanding of opponents. When a man has studied the history of the democrats and aristocrats of Corcyra, of the English and Irish, of the Jacobins and Anti-Jacobins, his political views may remain the same, but his political temper and his way of thinking about politics may have improved, if he is capable of receiving an impression.

And so, too, in a larger sphere than politics, a review of the process of historical evolution teaches a man to see his own age, with its peculiar ideals and interests, in proper perspective as one among other ages. If he can learn to understand that other ages had not only a different social and economic structure but correspondingly different ideals and interests from those of his own age, his mind will be veritably enlarged. I have hopes that ere long the Workers' Educational Association will have taught its historical students not to ask, "What was Shakespeare's attitude to Democracy?" and to perceive that the question no more admits of an answer than the inquiry, "What was Dante's attitude to Protestantism?" or, "What was Archimedes' attitude to the steam-engine?"

# CLIO, A MUSE

The study of cause and effect is by no means the only, and perhaps not the principal, means of broadening the mind. History does most to cure a man of political prejudice when it enables him, by reading about men or movements in the past, to understand points of view which he never saw before, and to respect ideals which he had formerly despised. Gardiner's *History of the Civil War* has done much to explain Englishmen to each other, by revealing the rich variety of our national life, far nobler than the unity of similitude. Forms of idealism, considerations of policy and wisdom, are acceptable, or at least comprehensible, when presented by the historian to minds which would reject them if they came from the political opponent or the professed sage.

But history should not only remove prejudice, it should breed enthusiasm. To many it is an important source of the ideas that inspire their lives. With the exception of a few creative minds, men are too weak to fly by their own unaided imagination beyond the circle of ideas that govern the world in which they are placed. And since the ideals of no one epoch can in themselves be sufficient as an interpretation of life, it is fortunate that the student of the past can draw upon the purest springs of ancient thought and feeling. Men will join in associations to propagate the old-new idea, and to recast society again in the ancient mould, as when the study of Plutarch and the ancient historians rekindled the breath of liberty and of civic virtue in modern Europe; as when in our own day men attempt to revive mediæval ideals of religious or of corporate life, or to rise to the Greek standard of the individual. We may like or dislike such revivals, but at least they bear witness to the potency of history as something quite other than a science. And, outside the circle of these larger influences, history supplies us each with private ideals, only too varied and too numerous for complete realization. One may aspire to the best characteristics of a man of Athens, or a citizen of Rome; a Churchman of the twelfth century, or a Reformer of the sixteenth; a Cavalier of the old school, or a Puritan of the independent party; a Radical of the time of Castle-reagh, or a public servant of the time of Peel. Still more are individual great men the model and inspiration of the smaller. It is difficult to appropriate the essential qualities of these old people under new conditions; but whatever we study with strong loving conception, and admire as a thing good in itself and not merely good for its purpose or its age, we do in some measure absorb.

This presentation of ideals and heroes from other ages is perhaps the most important among the educative functions of history. For this purpose, even more than for the purpose of teaching political wisdom, it is requisite that the events should be both written and read with intellectual passion. Truth itself will be the gainer, for those by whom history was enacted were in their day passionate.

Another educative function of history is to enable the reader to comprehend the historical aspect of literature proper. Literature can no doubt be enjoyed in its highest aspects even if the reader is ignorant of history. But on those terms it cannot be enjoyed completely, and much of it cannot be enjoyed at all. For much of literature is allusion, either definite or implied. And the allusions, even of the Victorian age, are by this time historical. For example, the last half-dozen stanzas of Browning's *Old Pictures in Florence*, the fifth stanza of his *Lovers' Quarrel*, and half his wife's best poems are already meaningless unless we know something of the Continental history of that day. Political authors like Burke, Sydney Smith and Courier, the prose of Milton, one half of Swift, the best of Dryden, and the best of Byron (his satires and letters) are enjoyed, *ceteris paribus*, in exact proportion to the amount we know of the history of their times. And since allusions to classical history and mythology, and even to the Bible, are no longer, as they used to be, familiar ground for all educated readers, there is all the more reason, in the interest of litera-ture, why allusions to modern history should be generally

understood. History and literature cannot be fully com-
prehended, still less fully enjoyed, except in connection
with one another. I confess I have little love either for
"histories of literature," or for chapters on "the literature
of the period," hanging at the end of history-books like
the tail from a cow. I mean, rather, that those who write
or read the history of a period should be soaked in its
literature, and that those who read or expound literature
should be soaked in history. The "scientific" view of
history that discouraged such interchange and desired the
strictest specialization by political historians has done much
harm to our latter-day culture. The mid-Victorians at any
rate knew better than that.

The substitution of a pseudo-scientific for a literary
atmosphere in historical circles has not only done much to
divorce history from the outside public, but has diminished
its humanizing power over its own devotees in school and
university. Not a few university teachers are already conscious of this, and are trying to remedy it, having seen that
historical "science" for the undergraduate means the text-
book—that is, the "crammer" in print. At one university
as I know, and at others I dare say, literature already
plays a greater part in historical teaching and reading than
it played some years ago. Historical students are now
encouraged to read the "literary" historians of old, who
were recently *taboo*, and still more to read the contemporary
literature of periods studied. But, for all that, there is much
leeway to be made up.

The value and pleasure of travel, whether at home or
abroad, is doubled by a knowledge of history. For places,
like books, have an interest or a beauty of association,
as well as an absolute or æsthetic beauty. The garden
front of St John's, Oxford, is beautiful to everyone; but
for the lover of history its outward charm is blent with
the intimate feelings of his own mind, with images of
that same College as it was during the Great Civil War.
Given over to the use of a Court whose days of royalty

were numbered, its walks and quadrangles were filled, as the end came near, with men and women learning to accept sorrow as their lot through life, the ambitious abandoning hope of power, the wealthy hardening themselves to embrace poverty, those who loved England preparing to sail for foreign shores, and lovers to be parted for ever. There they strolled through the garden, as the hopeless evenings fell, listening, at the end of all, while the siege guns broke the silence with ominous iteration. Behind the cannon on those low hills to northward were ranked the inexorable men who came to lay their hands on all this beauty, hoping to change it to strength and sterner virtue. And this was the curse of the victors, not to die, but to live, and almost to lose their awful faith in God, when they saw the Restoration, not of the old gaiety that was too gay for them and the old loyalty that was too loyal for them, but of corruption and selfishness that had neither country nor king. The sound of the Roundhead cannon has long ago died away, but still the silence of the garden is heavy with unalterable fate, brooding over besiegers and besieged, in such haste to destroy each other and permit only the vile to survive. St John's College is not mere stone and mortar, tastefully compiled, but an appropriate and mournful witness between those who see it now and those by whom it once was seen. And so it is, for the reader of history, with every ruined castle and ancient church throughout the wide, mysterious lands of Europe.

Battlefield hunting, a sport of which my dear master, Edward Bowen, was the most strenuous and successful patron, is one of the joys that history can afford to every walker and cyclist, and even to the man in the motor, if he can stir himself to get out to see the country through which he is whirled. The charm of an historic battlefield is its fortuitous character. Chance selected this field out of so many, that low wall, this gentle slope of grass, a windmill, a farm or straggling hedge, to turn the tide of war and decide the fate of nations and of creeds. Look on this scene, restored to its rustic sleep that was so rudely interrupted on that one day in all the ages; and looking, laugh at the "science of history." But for some honest soldier's pluck or luck in the decisive onslaught round yonder village spire, the lost cause would now be hailed as "the tide of inevitable tendency" that nothing could have turned aside! How charmingly remote and casual are such places as Rosbach and Valmy, Senlac and Marston Moor. Or take the case of Morat. There, over that green hill beneath the lowland firwood, the mountaineers from alp and glacier-foot swept on with thundering feet and bellowing war horns, and at sight of their levelled pikes the Burgundian chivalry, arrayed in all the gorgeous trappings of the Renaissance armourers, fled headlong into Morat lake down there. From that day forward, Swiss democracy, thrusting aside the Duke of Savoy, planted itself on the Genevan shore, and Europe, therefore, in the fullness of time, got Calvin and Rousseau. A fine chain of cause and effect, which I lay humbly at the feet of "science"!

The skilled game of identifying positions on a battlefield innocent of guides, where one must make out everything for oneself—best of all if no one has ever done it properly before — is almost the greatest of out-door intellectual pleasures.[1] But the solution of the military problem is not all. If the unsentimental tourist thinks of the men who fought there merely as pawns in a game of chess, if the moral issues of the war are unknown to him or indifferent, he loses half that he might have had. To be perfect, he must know and feel what kind of men they were who climbed the terraces at Calatafimi or stormed the rifle-pits on Missionary Ridge; who marched up to the stockade at Blenheim to the sound of fife and drum; who hacked at

---

[1] Let me recommend Mr Oman's *History of the Art of War* to would-be hunters of battlefields, if any of them do not know it. That work and Gardiner's *Civil War* will set them to work the right way on many of our best British battlefields. But when is Mr Oman's instructive and delightful book to be completed?

each other that evening on Marston Moor. And it is best of all when the battle decided something great that still has a claim on our gratitude.

As one who ardently desires the abolition of war, I regret that the well-meaning poet who sang long ago of "old Kaspar" was not historically better informed. To choose Blenheim as an example of a useless waste of blood and treasure was unfortunate, for it was one of the few battles thoroughly worth fighting. "What they killed each other for"! Why, to save us all from belonging to the French king, who had at that moment got Spain, Italy, Belgium and half Germany in his pocket. To prevent Western Europe from sinking under a Czardom inspired by the Jesuits. To make the "Sun King's" system of despotism and religious persecution look so weak and silly beside English freedom that all the philosophers and wits of the new century would make mock of it. Who would have listened to Voltaire and Rousseau, or even to Montesquieu, if Blenheim had gone the other way, and the Grand Monarch had been gathered in glory to the grave? We are always telling ourselves "how England saved Europe" from Napoleon — truly enough, though incidentally we handed her over to taskmasters scarcely less abominable. But we hear very little of "how England saved Europe" from Louis XIV. How many Englishmen have ever visited Blenheim? It is as good a field as Waterloo, though a little farther off in time and space, and it still lies undisfigured by monuments, its villages and fields still as old Kaspar knew them, between the wooded hills above and the reedy islands of slow-moving Danube, into which Tallard's Horse were driven headlong on that day of deliverance to mankind.

In this vexed question, whether history is an art or a science, let us call it both or call it neither. For it has an element of both. It is not in guessing at historical "cause and effect" that science comes in; but in collecting and weighing evidence as to facts, something of the scientific spirit is required for an historian, just as it is for a detective or a politician.

To my mind there are three distinct functions of history, that we may call the *scientific*, the *imaginative* or *speculative*, and the *literary*. First comes what we may call the *scientific*, if we confine the word to this narrow but vital function, the day-labour that every historian must well and truly perform if he is to be a serious member of his profession —the accumulation of facts and the sifting of evidence. "Every great historian has been his own Dry-as-dust," said Stubbs, and quoted Carlyle as the example. Then comes the *imaginative* or *speculative*, when he plays with the facts that he has gathered, selects and classifies them, and makes his guesses and generalizations. And last but not least comes the *literary* function, the exposition of the results of science and imagination in a form that will attract and educate our fellow-countrymen. For this last process I use the word "literature," because I wish to lay greater stress than modern historians are willing to do, both on the difficulty and also on the importance of planning and writing a powerful narrative of historical events. Arrangement, composition and style are not as easily acquired as the art of typewriting. Literature never helps any man at his task until, to obtain her services, he is willing to be her faithful apprentice. Writing is not, therefore, a secondary but one of the primary tasks of the historian.

Another reason why I prefer to use the word "literature" for the expository side of the historian's work is, that literature itself is in our day impoverished by these attempts to cut it off from scholarship and serious thought. It would be disastrous if the reading public came to think of literature not as a grave matron, but as a mere *fille de joie*. Until near the end of the nineteenth century literature was held to mean not only plays, novels and *belles lettres*, but all writing that rose above a certain standard of excellence. Novels, if they are bad enough, are not literature. Pamphlets, if they are good enough, are literature—for example, the pamphlets of Milton, Swift and Burke. Huxley's essays and Maine's treatises are literature. Even Maitland's expositions of mediæval law are literature. Maitland, indeed, wrote well rather by force of genius, by natural brilliancy, than by any great attention paid to composition, form and style. But for us little people it is just that conscious attention to book-planning, composition and style that I would advocate.

All students who may some day write history, and in any case will be judges of what is written, should be encouraged to make a critical study of past masters of English historical literature. Yet there were many places a little time ago where it was tacitly accepted as passable and even praiseworthy in an historical student to know nothing of the great English historians prior to Stubbs. And, for all I know, there are such places still.

In France historical writing is on a higher level than in England, because the Frenchman is taught to write his own language as part of his school curriculum. The French *savant* is bred, if not born, a prose writer. Consequently when he arrives at manhood he already writes well by habit. The recent union effected in France of German standards of research with this native power of composition and style has produced a French historical school that turns out yearly a supply of history-books at once scholarly and delightful. Of course any attempt to assimilate English history to the uniform French pattern would be as foolish as the recent attempt to assimilate it to the German. We must be ourselves. All our scholars cannot be expected to write with the smooth cadence and lucid sequence of idea that is the hall-mark of the commonest French writers. But many more of us, if we held it our duty to labour at writing well, would soon rival French stylists; and not seldom, in the future as in the past, some master of our language might arise who would surpass them far.

French is in any case an easier language to manipulate

than our own. Apart even from the handicaps in our system of education, it is probably harder for the English than for the French historian to write prose up to a certain level of excellence. But if that is so, it is only an added reason for a greater expenditure of effort on prose composition and book-planning by the rising generation of English historians. It is very difficult to write good English prose; and to tell a learned story as it should be told requires both intellectual and artistic effort. The idea that history is a "soft option" for classics and science still subtly operates to keep some of the very best men out of the history schools. This would cease altogether to be the case if it were universally recognized that history is not merely the accumulation and interpretation of facts—hard enough that in itself!—but involves besides the whole art of book composition and prose style. Life is short, art is long, but history is longest, for it is art added to scholarship.

The idea that histories which are delightful to read must be the work of superficial temperaments, and that a crabbed style betokens a deep thinker or conscientious worker, is the reverse of the truth. What is easy to read has been difficult to write. The labour of writing and rewriting, correcting and recorrecting, is the due exacted by every good book from its author, even if he know from the beginning exactly what he wants to say. A limpid style is invariably the result of hard labour, and the easily flowing connection of sentence with sentence and paragraph with paragraph has always been won by the sweat of the brow.

Now in the case of history all this artistic work is superimposed on the labours of scholarship, themselves enough to fill a lifetime. The historical architect must quarry his own stones and build with his own hands. Division of labour is possible in only a limited degree. No wonder then that there have been so few historians really on a level with the opportunities of their great themes, and that except Gibbon every one of them is imperfect either in science or in art. The double task, hard as it is, we little people must shoulder as best we may, in the temporary absence of giants. And if the finest intellects of the rising generation can be made to realize how hard is the task of history, more of them will become historians.

Writing history well is no child's play. The rounding of every sentence and of every paragraph has to be made consistent with a score of facts, some of them known only to the author, some of them perhaps discovered or remembered by him at the last moment to the entire destruction of some carefully erected artistic structure. In such cases there is an undoubted temptation to the artist to neglect such small, inconvenient pieces of truth. That, I think, is the one strong point in the scholar's outcry against "literary history"; but if we wish to swim we must go into the water, and there is little use in cloistered virtue, nor much more in cloistered scholarship. In history, as it is now written, art is sacrificed to science ten times for every time that science is sacrificed to art.

It will be well here, in our search after the true English tradition, to hold briefly in review the history of history, so far as our own island is concerned.

Clarendon was the father of English history. The Chroniclers and Shakespeare, Bacon and Sir Walter Raleigh had prepared the way, but Clarendon, by his *History of the Great Rebellion*, established the English tradition, which lasted for two hundred years: the tradition, namely, that history was a part of the national literature, and was meant for the education and delight of all who read books. Like Thucydides and Philippe de Comines before him, Clarendon wrote a chronicle of great events in which he had himself taken part. For in those early days, whether in ancient Athens, mediæval France or Stuart England, there was no large body of trained antiquaries collecting, sorting and studying the documents of the past; and therefore history, if it was

# CLIO, A MUSE

to be in the least detailed, and even partially reliable, must needs concern itself only with contemporary affairs. That was a grave limitation and disadvantage; yet Clarendon's partisan history of his own time was raised by the dignity of its author's mind, and the grave majestic eloquence of his style, into a treasure-house whence five successive generations of the English governing class, both the Tories who agreed and the Whigs who disagreed with his principles, drew their first deep lessons in the art of politics and in the management of men, their pride in the institutions of the country which they were called upon to govern, and their detailed knowledge of the great events in the past by which those institutions had been shaped and inspired.

During the century that followed Clarendon, many people wrote political memoirs and "histories of my own time," modelled more or less successfully upon his great exemplar. Of these, Burnet's is one of the best known. By means of this Clarendonian literature, most educated persons were admirably trained in the history of the earlier and later Stuart Revolutions.

After this Clarendonian epoch, of which the best products were contemporary history and political memoirs, there followed, in the middle of the eighteenth century, attempts to collect evidence and write reliable history about events in the past altogether outside the author's own experience. This movement, associated with the names of Hume and Robertson, was rendered possible by the antiquarian activity and scientific spirit of the "age of reason."

The new school quickly culminated in the perfect genius of Gibbon. I call his genius perfect because, though limited, it had no faults in its kind. As all historians should aspire to do, Gibbon united accuracy with art. If proof is needed that a literary history may be accurate, it is found in Gibbon. His scientific work of sifting all the evidence that was in his day available has suffered singularly little from criticism, even in our archæological age when the spade corrects the

164

pen. His literary art was no less perfect, and was the result of infinite pains to become a great writer. If Gibbon had taken as little trouble about writing as later historians, his volumes would have been as little read, and would have perished as quickly as theirs.

But Gibbon had his limitations, though his science and his art were alike perfect of their kind. His limitations were those of his age. His friends and contemporaries, the Encyclopædist philosophers, prepared the successes and errors of the French Revolution by their *a priori* conception of society in all countries as a blank sheet for the pen of pure reason. Like them, Gibbon conceived mankind to be essentially the same in all ages and in all countries. In all ages and in all countries his sceptical eye detected the same classes, the same passions, the same follies. For him there is always and everywhere the ruler, the philosopher, the mob, the aristocrat, the fanatic and the augur, alike in ancient Rome or modern France and England. He did not perceive that the thoughts of men, as well as the framework of society, differ from age to age. The long centuries of diverse human experience, which he chronicled with such passionless equanimity, look all much the same in the cold, classical light of his reason.

But Gibbon was scarcely in the grave when a genius arose in Scotland who once and probably for ever transformed mankind's conception of itself from the classical to the romantic, from the uniform to the variegated. Gibbon's cold, classical light was replaced by the rich mediæval hues of Walter Scott's stained glass. To Scott each age, each profession, each country, each province had its own manners, its own dress, its own way of thinking, talking and fighting. To Scott a man is not so much a human being as a type produced by special environment, whether it be a border farmer, a mediæval abbot, a cavalier, a covenanter, a Swiss pikeman, or an Elizabethan statesman. No doubt Scott exaggerated his theme, as all innovators are wont to do. But he did more than any professional historian to make mankind advance towards a true conception of history, for it was he who first perceived that the history of mankind is not simple but complex, that history never repeats itself but ever creates new forms differing according to time and place. The great antiquarian and novelist showed historians that history must be living, many-coloured and romantic if it is to be a true mirror of the past.[1] Macaulay, who was a boy while Scott's poems and novels were coming out, and who knew much of them by heart, was not slow to learn this lesson.

Then followed the Victorian age, the period when history in England reached the height of its popularity and of its influence on the national mind. In the eighteenth century the educated class had been numerically very small, though it had been a most powerful and discriminating patron of letters and learning, above all of history. No country house of any pretension was without its Clarendon, Robertson, Hume and Gibbon, as can be seen in many an old neglected private library to-day, where now the inhabitants, in the intervals of golf and motoring, wear off the edge of their intellects on magazines and bad novels.

In the Victorian era education and reading were beginning to spread from the few to the many, and the modern habit of reading mainly trash had not yet set in. Therefore it was a golden age for all sorts of literature, including history. In the earlier half of the Victorian period, when Arnold and Milman, Grote and Merivale flourished, the American Motley and Prescott were household words over here as well as in their own country. It is hard for us to conceive the degree to which serious history affected our grandfathers. History no longer, as in the eighteenth century, confined its influence to the upper

---

[1] Both as literature and as social history his Scottish novels are his best. They are the real truth about the land which " the Shirra " knew so well, whereas *Ivanhoe*, *Quentin Durward* and *Woodstock* are only the guesswork of learning and genius, in every way less valuable now than they once were. But when first published, those novels, no less than the Scottish novels, revealed to an astonished world the reality and variety of past ages.

classes. I have often seen Motley's *Dutch Republic* on the ancestral shelf of a country cottage or an inn parlour, where only magazines and novels are now added to the pile.

Above all others there were Macaulay and Carlyle. Of Carlyle I have spoken already, as an historian not indeed to be imitated directly, but to be admired and studied because he was a man of genius, and because he was everything good and bad that we modern historians are not. Of Macaulay, too, something must here be said, because an undistinguishing condemnation of him used to be the shibboleth of that school of English historians who destroyed the habit of reading history among their fellow-countrymen.

In "arrangement" — that is to say, in the planning of the book, in the way subject leads on to subject and paragraph to paragraph—Macaulay's *History* has no equal, and ought to be carefully studied by everyone who intends to write a narrative history. His "style," the actual form of his sentences, ought not to be imitated, partly because it is open to criticism, still more because it was his own and inimitable. But if anybody could imitate his "arrangement" and then invent a "style" as effective for our age as Macaulay's was for his, he would be able to make the best results of the modern history school familiar to hundreds of thousands, and influential on all the higher thought and feeling of the day.

People have been taught to suppose that Macaulay's Whiggism was his worst historical fault. I wish it had been. His real fault was an inherent overcertainty of temper, flattered by the easy victories of his youth. He never met serious historical criticism or resistance until he was too old to change.[1] But in his view of history he was not such a

---

[1] The same may be said of other great Victorians—Carlyle and Ruskin in particular. Our own age is too critical to be highly favourable to creative genius, that is in regions where there are any literary or intellectual standards at all. But the early Victorian age had not enough criticism to trim the mighty plants that grew in it so wild. Matthew Arnold came twenty years too late for this purpose.

Whig as he has been painted. Not only does he perpetually fall foul of the Whigs on minor issues, but he censures them on the point of their main policy at the end of Charles II.'s reign—the candidature of Monmouth for the throne. And again, when having beaten Louis to his knees they refused to make peace with him, their supposed apologist writes: " It seems to us that on the great question which divided England during the last four years of Anne's reign the Tories were in the right and the Whigs were in the wrong." This position he maintained against his Tory friend and fellow-historian, Lord Mahon. Shaftesbury, the founder of the Whig party, is treated by this " Whig historian " with marked animosity, and even unfairness. Shaftesbury is accused of advising " the Stop on the Exchequer," which, in fact, he opposed, and is never given credit for any disinterested motive. No doubt Shaftesbury, like most of the statesmen of that era, was a very bad man, but modern historians differ from Macaulay in ascribing to the first Whig some qualities not wholly devilish. It is clear that in this case at least Macaulay was misled not by his " Whiggism " but by a too simple-hearted hatred of knavery and by the artistic instinct to paint a study in black. And from this it is fair arguing that in some other cases where the paint is laid on too thick, the temptation to which he has yielded has not been political but artistic. Antithesis was dear to him not only in the composition of his sentences but in the delineation of his characters. It was with him a matter not of politics but of unconscious instinct to contrast as vividly as possible the selfishness with the genius of Marlborough. But, unfortunately, he lived to complete only the least important and pleasing half of the picture. He had blocked in only too well the black background, but died before he came to the red coat and eagle eye of the victor of Blenheim. If Macaulay had lived another five years, Marlborough would now enjoy the full meed of admiration and gratitude still denied to him by his countrymen's little knowledge of what he did.

# CLIO, A MUSE

Mommsen and Treitschke, at whose German shrines we have been instructed to sacrifice the traditions of English history, were partisans, the one of Roman, the other of Prussian Cæsarism, more blind and bitter than Macaulay was of middle-class parliamentary government. Macaulay's historical sympathy was, more often than not, aroused by courage, honesty or literary merit, irrespective of party or creed. But Mommsen's treatment of Cæsar's enemies is an outrage against good sense and feeling. Compare his unworthy sneers at Cicero with Macaulay's reverence for the genius of Dryden and Dr Johnson, the piety and moral courage of Jeremy Collier, the valour of Claverhouse at Killiecrankie or Sarsfield at Limerick. Macaulay's generosity of mind—within its natural limitations—the glow of pride with which he speaks of anything and anybody who has ennobled the annals of our country or of European civilization, his indignation with knaves, poltroons and bullies of all parties and creeds, his intense and infectious pleasure in the annals of the past, rendered his *History of England* an education in patriotism, humanity and statesmanship. The book made men proud of their country, it made them understand her institutions, how they had come into existence and how liberty and order had been won by the wear and tear of contending factions. His Whiggism in the historical field consisted of a belief in religious toleration and parliamentary government—principles in which an historian has just as good a right to believe as in absolutism and persecution.

His errors as an historian sprang not from his opinions on Church and State, which, right or wrong, were commonplace enough, being very much those of a moderate free-trade Unionist of the present day. Neither did his errors spring from any limitation in his reading, which was deeper than that of any English historian in his own time. Neither was he lacking in general equipment as an historian: he was a very good linguist; he was a man of the world and accustomed to great public affairs; and he was a fine historical lawyer—Maitland one day, in praising Macaulay, said to me that he was always right in the frequent discussions of legal points that characterize his *History*. It was not then from his politics, nor from lack of reading his authorities, nor from lack of general equipment, that his errors sprang. They sprang from three sources. First, from a too great reliance on his miraculous memory and an insufficient use of notes. Secondly, from too great certainty of temper, a combined precision and limitation of intellectual outlook which annoyed men like Matthew Arnold and John Morley in the more sceptical age that followed his own, and will continue in a less degree to annoy most of us, though we can now afford to be more fair towards him than were those first rebels against his once so formidable power. And, lastly, he had a disastrous habit of attributing motives: he was never content to say that a man did this or that, and leave his motives to conjecture; he must always needs analyse all that had passed through the mind of his *dramatis personæ* as if he were the God who had created them. In this habit of always attributing motives as if they were known matters of fact, Macaulay is " a warning to the young."

In his own day, and for a generation after his death, his *History of England* was read by hundreds of thousands of his countrymen, and it made our history and institutions familiar to all the world. If I have been right in arguing that the ultimate value of history is not scientific but educational, then the service that he rendered to Clio by making her known to the people was the most essential and pertinent of all.

Indeed, in the period immediately following on Macaulay's death, History seemed to be coming to her own. His works and Carlyle's continued to be read, and those of Motley, Froude, Lecky, Green, Symonds, Spencer Walpole, Leslie Stephen, John Morley, and others, carried on the tradition that history was related to literature. The foundations of a broad, national culture, based upon knowledge of our history and pride in England's past, seemed to be securely laid. The coming generation of historians had only to build upon the great foundation of popularity laid for them by their predecessors, erecting whatever new structures of political or other opinion they wished, but preserving the basis of literary history, of history as the educator of the people. But they preferred to destroy the foundations, to sever the tie between history and the reading public. They gave it out that Carlyle and Macaulay were "literary historians" and therefore ought not to be read. The public, hearing thus on authority that they had been "exposed" and were "unsound," ceased to read them—or anybody else. Hearing that history was a science they left it to scientists. The craving for lighter literature which characterized the new generation combined with the academic dead-set against literary history to break the public of its old habit of reading history-books.

At the present moment the state of affairs seems to me both better and worse than it was twenty years ago when I came to Cambridge as an undergraduate, and was solemnly instructed by the author of *Ecce Homo* that Macaulay and Carlyle did not know what they were writing about, and that "literary history" was a thing of naught. The present generation of historians at Oxford and Cambridge have ceased, so far as I am aware, to preach this fanatical crusade; they recognize that history has more than one function, and are ready to welcome various kinds of historians. There is therefore much hope for the future, because ideas on such matters in the end spread down from the universities to the schools and the country, and gradually permeate opinion far away.

But, for the present, things in the country at large are scarcely better than they were twenty years ago. We are still suffering the consequence of the anti-literary campaign carried on by the historical chiefs of the recent past. Schoolmasters, private tutors and other purveyors of general ideas are often a generation behind the time, though striving hard to say and do what they imagine to be the "correct thing." The camp-followers of the historical army of to-day sometimes seek an easy reputation by repeating as the last word of wisdom the shibboleths of the anti-literary movement, which appears to me to be regarded as somewhat out of date in the centre of things at the universities. I have more than once come across the case of schoolboys being positively forbidden to read Macaulay, who, whether he be a guide for grown-ups or not, is certainly an admirable stimulus to the sluggish youthful mind, none too apt to develop enthusiasm either for history or for literature. And I have known a history-book condemned by a reviewer on the ground that it would read aloud well! Often, when recommending some readable and stimulating history, I have been answered: "Oh! but has not his view been proved incorrect?" Or, "Is he not out of date? I am told one ought not to read him now." And so, the "literary historians" being ruled out by authority, the would-be student declines on some wretched text-book, or else reads nothing at all.

This attitude of mind is not only disastrous in its consequences to the intellectual life of the country, but radically unsound in its premises. For it assumes that history — "scientific history" — has "proved" certain views to be true and others to be false. Now history can prove the truth or falsehood of facts but not of opinions. When a man begins with the pompous formula, "The verdict of history is . . ." suspect him at once, for he is merely dressing up his own opinions in big words. Fifty years ago the "verdict of history" was mainly Whig and Protestant; twenty years ago mainly Tory and Anglo-Catholic; to-day it is, fortunately, much more variegated. Each juror now brings in his own verdict—generally with a recommendation of everyone to mercy. There is even some danger that history may encourage the idea that all sides in the quarrels of the past were equally right and equally wrong.

There is no "verdict of history" other than the private opinion of the individual. And no one historian can possibly see more than a fraction of the truth; if he sees all sides, he will probably not see very deeply into any one of them.

The only way in which a reader can arrive at a valuable judgment on some historical period is to read several good histories, whether contemporary or modern, written from several different points of view, and to think about them for himself.[1] But too often the reading of good books and the exercise of individual judgment are shirked, while some vacuous text-book is favoured on the ground that it is "impartial" and "up-to-date." But no book, least of all a text-book, affords a short cut to the historical truth. The truth is not grey, it is black and white in patches. And there is nothing black or white but thinking makes it so.

The dispassionateness of the historian is a quality which it is easy to value too highly, and it should not be confused with the really indispensable qualities of accuracy and good faith. We cannot be at too great pains to see that our passion burns pure, but we must not extinguish the flame. Dispassionateness—*nil admirari*—may betray the most gifted historian into missing some vital truth in his subject. In Creighton's treatment of Luther, all that he says is both fair and accurate, yet from Creighton alone you would not guess that Luther was a great man or the German Reformation a stirring and remarkable movement. The few pages on Luther in Carlyle's *Heroes* are the proper complement to this excessively dispassionate history. The two should be read together.

Acton is sometimes thought of by the outside public as an impartial and dispassionate historian. Yet it was his favourite doctrine that history ought always to be passing moral judgments—generally very severe ones. On every subject that he treated historically he showed himself a

---

[1] Biography is very useful for this purpose. The lives of rival statesmen, warriors and thinkers, provided they are good books, are often the quickest route to the several points of view that composed the life of an epoch. *Ceteris paribus*, a single biography is more likely to mislead than a history of the period, but several biographies are often more deeply instructive than a single history.

strong partisan, although his "party" in Church and State seems to have consisted of only one member. Nor was he deficient in the artistic sense: his lectures at Cambridge were dramatic performances, with surprises, limelights and curtains. He dearly liked to "make your flesh creep." No doubt these qualities sometimes misled him,[1] but if he had not had in him ethical passion and artistic sense he would by now be forgotten. Lord Acton's opinions are not likely to be accepted by anyone *en masse*, and for my part I accept only a small portion of them; yet I firmly believe that his opinions and the zeal with which he held them were the spiritual force that made him not only a great man but a great historian.

In the Victorian age the influence of historians and of historical thinkers did much to form the ideas of the new era, though less, of course, than the poets and novelists. To-day almost all that is characteristic in the mind of the young generation is derived from novelists and playwrights. It is natural and right that novelists and playwrights (provided we can count among them poets!) should do most to form the type of mind of any generation, but a little steadying from other influences like history might be a good leaven in modern gospels and movements.

The public has ceased to watch with any interest the appearance of historical works, good or bad. *The Cambridge Modern History* is indeed bought by the yard to decorate bookshelves, but it is regarded like the *Encyclopædia Britannica* as a work of reference; its mere presence in the library is enough. Publishers, meanwhile, palm off on the public books manufactured for them in Grub Street—"publishers' books," which are neither literature nor first-hand scholarship. This is the type generically known as "Criminal Queens of History," spicy memoirs of dead courts and pseudo-biographical chatter about Napoleon and his family, how many eggs he ate and how many miles he drove a day.

---

[1] See *Edinburgh Review*, April 1907.

And Lady Hamilton is a great stand-by. The public understands that this kind of prurient journalism is history lightly served up for the general appetite, whereas serious history is a sacred thing pinnacled afar on frozen heights of science, not to be approached save after a long novitiate.

By itself, this picture of our present discontents would be exaggerated and one-sided. There is much truth in it, I fear; but on the other hand there is much good in the present and more hope in the future. For a new public has arisen, a vast democracy of all classes from " public " school and " council " school alike, taught to read but not knowing what to read; men and women of this new democracy of intellect, from millionaire to mechanic, refuse to be bored in a world where the means of amusement have been brought to every door; but, subject to that condition, the best of them, the natural leaders of the rest, are athirst for thought and knowledge if only it be presented to them in an interesting form.

To meet this demand, to grasp this opportunity, several great movements are now afoot. The new historical teaching at universities and public schools is one of them; the Workers' Educational Association is another; a third is the movement for short outline books written by the best specialists in the most popular style they can master. The Home University Library is the principal of these—organized by Mr Herbert Fisher, and supported by books from half-a-dozen others among our very best historians.

All this is magnificent. I only hope that yet another movement, tending in another way to meet the opportunities of the new age, will also gradually come about. I mean that not only these small handbooks but the main works of our historical scholars should be written not merely for the perusal of brother historians but for the best portion of the general public — in other words, that they should be written as literature. And, above all, that the art of narrative in history should be treated with much greater reverence, and be accorded a larger portion of the effort and brain-power which our modern historians dispend so generously, and in other respects so fruitfully, in the service of Clio.

If, as we have so often been told with such glee, the days of "literary history" have gone never to return, the world is left the poorer. Self-congratulation on this head is but the mood of the shorn fox in the fable. History as literature has a function of its own, and we suffer to-day from its atrophy. Fine English prose, when devoted to the serious exposition of fact and argument, has a glory of its own, and the civilization that boasts only of creative fiction on one side and science on the other may be great but is not complete. Prose is seldom equal to poetry either in the fine manipulation of words or in emotional content, yet it can have great value in both those kinds, and when to these it adds the intellectual exactness of argument or narrative that poetry does not seek to rival, then is it sovereign in its own domain. To read sustained and magnificent historical narrative educates the mind and the character; some even whose natures, craving the definite, seldom respond to poetry, find in such writing the highest pleasure that they know. Unfortunately, historians of literary genius have never been plentiful, and we are told that there will never be any more. Certainly we shall have to wait for them, but let us also wish for them and work for them. If we confess that we lack something, and cease to make a merit of our chief defect, if we encourage the rising generation to work at the art of construction and narrative as a part of the historian's task, we may at once get a better level of historical writing, and our children may live to enjoy modern Gibbons, judicious Carlyles and sceptical Macaulays.

# THE PRESENT POSITION OF HISTORY [1]

THERE are, it is probable, some persons here to-day who were present at the inaugural lecture given by Lord Acton more than thirty years ago. If so, they remember how its incomparable learning, its cosmopolitan outlook, and its moral and philosophic power, made us feel that we had found a master who soon proved to be a friend. Its opening sentences closely touched his audience when he told us that as a young man he had set his heart on coming up to this university, but that, after being refused admittance at three colleges, he had abandoned the attempt in despair. My own early relation to Cambridge is very different. For ten years she was a most indulgent mother to my irresponsible youth. From her I learnt what freedom and what friendship mean. I left her of my own choice, to follow yet more freely my own devices, according to plans I had formed in her courts and groves. And now, after twenty-five years, I return, welcomed back here with the same indulgence that I knew of old. May I prove worthy to say to *Alma Mater*:

> " Feel, where my life broke off from thine,
> How fresh the splinters keep and fine,
> Only a touch and we combine ! "

As a freshman, in 1893, I had the privilege of being taught by Lord Acton's predecessor, Sir John Seeley, who had himself succeeded Charles Kingsley as Professor in 1869, shortly before the history tripos came into existence.[2] Seeley

[1] Inaugural lecture as Regius Professor, delivered at Cambridge, 27th October 1927.
[2] The law and history tripos began in 1870; the history tripos proper in 1875. That year ten students were examined in it; in 1927 over three hundred, if we reckon both parts of the tripos.

was a great publicist as well as historian. He held a political doctrine applicable to his own day, and was eager to support it with arguments and illustrations drawn from history. Such political interests may be the inspiration or the poison of historical work, according to circumstances. Often they are both inspiration and poison at once. In Seeley's case I think the results were fortunate. For in his political enthusiasm to arouse the later subjects of Queen Victoria to a consciousness of their Imperial responsibilities he drew the attention of historians to the tale of British overseas policy and enterprise, till then a subsidiary and neglected branch of study. In lecturing here on *The Expansion of England*, he expanded history as well. We have travelled far along that road since then, in history no less than in politics.

Unlike Seeley, I am not a publicist. I make no pretension to contribute anything drawn from history to the world's stock of wisdom and unwisdom in dealing with the affairs of to-day. Only I believe that the truth about the past, if taught or read with broad human sympathy, can give a noble education to the mind of the student, not only in politics, but in all kinds of civic and social relationship, and even in the domain of personal, religious and ethical ideals. History does not make men Guelphs or Ghibellines. But, if rightly studied, it makes them better Guelphs or better Ghibellines. If wrongly studied it may end in filling the streets with blood, and the countryside with trenches and bursting shells. The war of 1870 was ascribed by some to the historical writings of Thiers, and the greater catastrophe of our own era to those of Treitschke. There was probably an element of truth in these charges. But, if rightly taught, the annals of mankind cultivate a more intelligent patriotism that respects the claims of others.

But do not misunderstand me. History cannot rightly be used as propaganda even in the best of causes. It is not rightly taught by selecting such facts as will, it is hoped, point towards some patriotic or international moral. It is

178

rightly taught by the disclosure, so far as is humanly possible, of the truth about the past in all its variety and many-sidedness, in its national and international aspects, and in many other aspects besides these two. Your pupil or your reader may find modern applications for himself, if he is so disposed. But it is not the modern applications that are the root of the matter; the value of history to the solution of present-day problems is indirect, and lies in the training of the student's mind by the dispassionate study of some closed episode in human affairs.

History is the open Bible: we historians are not priests to expound it infallibly: our function is to teach people to read it and to reflect upon it for themselves. If we were to set up for infallible, our own divisions would speedily confound the claim. Men talk, indeed, of the " verdict of history," but on most points of real interest that verdict is not unanimous, and is constantly being reversed. The " verdict of history " is one thing in France, another in Germany; one thing in the England of 1840, another in 1890, yet a third thing to-day. Action and reaction is as much the method of historical as of political progress. For example, within two generations the general attitude towards the English Reformation and the Industrial Revolution respectively, displayed by the leading historical scholars on those subjects, has more than once undergone marked change, like the slow, constant swinging of a pendulum. Yet the figure of the pendulum is not to be pressed too close, for reactions in historical opinion never go back precisely to the old point. Each generation of historians reacts against its predecessor in certain respects, but the thought and learning of the previous generation has always left some mark that cannot be obliterated in the palimpsest of history.

Learning is indeed a necessary condition to the discovery of historical truth, but it is no infallible guide to just historical judgments. For since the most learned historians often hold widely divergent views, it is evident that they cannot all be right. What common judgment would you get out of Klopp and Legrelle, Froude and James Gairdner? There is another class of historical judge, who sees safety in the compromising policy of Solomon, and divides the baby exactly in half. But there are many cases in which this procedure may be a mortal error. There is, in fact, no golden rule by which to read history aright.

Indeed a large part of the business of historians consists in correcting and supplementing one another. I say "supplementing" because an accurate but one-sided history may, by its omissions, mislead the public far more than a less accurate and less learned record that presents several sides of the case. But because there are many historians, truth does slowly and partially emerge.

Truth is perpetually being brought to light, not merely by writers of cool and detached temper, but also by the rival contributions of those who ardently espouse opposite sides in some historic cause. The past was full of passion, and passion is therefore one element in historic truth. Sympathy is a necessary part of understanding. Carlyle helped as much as Gardiner to elucidate the forgotten truth about the English Puritan era and the character and career of Cromwell, about whom generations of dispassionate historians, Whig as well as Tory, had unerringly missed the point.

And so, by various processes, conducted by historians of very different types, the wide margins of error and ignorance are reduced. Each year there is less ground available for the perpetual misrepresentations employed by creed, class and race; and although these will be with us always, something nearer to common ground is being won for men of reason, honesty and good will.

Those, however, who believe that history can supply complete or final "verdicts," forget, I think, the immensity and complexity of the ground to be covered. Any historic event—say, for example, the course of the English or of the French Revolution—would involve, if it were traced with complete scientific accuracy, the life-histories of many millions of men and women, nearly all of them utterly unknown to us to-day, yet each of them once a living personality, growing and changing under stress of circumstances and influences constantly in flux.  The totality of past experience and action among European men, or even in the English nation alone in a limited period of years, presents a theme so vast and so intricate that we can discuss it at all only by making certain formulæ or historical generalizations, which cover and shroud the variety and richness of the past.  On the shore where Time casts up its stray wreckage we gather corks and broken planks, whence much indeed may be argued and more guessed; but what the great ship was that has gone down into the deep, that we shall never see.

Indeed, one of the attractions in studying the past is the sense which that study awakes that far more has been doomed to irrevocable oblivion than the little that anyone can ever know.  That touches the imagination.  Text-books and all manner of cramming for examinations, with their neat, necessary docketings of eras and movements, diminish the sense of the unplumbed and uncharted wastes of history.  It is nourished by turning over original documents, old letters that lack the answer, diaries like Pepys', memoirs like Hickey's.  It is nourished also by reading great histories by remarkable writers, and by meditating upon them. Maitland, for instance, added greatly to our knowledge of the Middle Ages, but none the less he thrilled us with a most exciting sense of our ignorance of the real thoughts and motives of men in those far-off days, even of our English ancestors who walked the lanes we tread.  By opening here and there a brilliantly lighted peep-hole into the blackness of the remote past, to show us some village tragi-comedy or the inside of some mediæval lawyer's brain at work, Maitland revealed to us indeed many definite things; but he showed us also that the past, when we suddenly see a piece of it close at hand, was so different from the present that we no longer feel confidence in reconstructing the thirteenth century from the analogy of our own experience and observation in a different age.

It is difficult to set bounds to the scope of history. It is concerned with every activity of man. Seeley mistook when he argued for its limitation to politics, if that was what he meant when he said that history was " past politics." Even if our sole end in view were to understand past politics—a dreary limitation—we should have first to study past economics, past religion, past jurisprudence, past social life and custom : for past politics were the mere outward form and flourish of these and many other activities of human life of old. If we studied past politics in isolation they would be emptied of their motive and meaning as surely as ecclesiastical history loses its reality when written apart from the social, intellectual and political history of the age in question. A purely political narrative of the struggle of King and Parliament in England, a purely ecclesiastical Life of Becket, Calvin or Laud, read like the chronicles of Cloud-Cuckoo-Land. History must be many-sided, because human life has many sides. We may and must cut it into sections for the convenience of our studies ; but to know the causes of events we must reassemble the parts.

Indeed, it so happened that in the latter years of Seeley's professorship, history, not least here at Cambridge, was starting forward on one of its periodic marches into new regions, notably at that time into regions economic and legal. Cunningham was making economic history a university subject, and the genius of Maitland was beginning to shine in upon old legal papers and muniment-rooms on which the dust of six centuries had been allowed to collect. Yet although there were great movements afoot, and great minds at work, collectively we history men were few in number and a feeble folk, living in the shadow of the great schools of classics, mathematics and science, when I first knew Cambridge between the two Jubilees of Queen Victoria.

OF HISTORY

Yet time was on our side, and a great transference of numbers from classics might even then have been prophesied. Rapid development was certain, but it might easily have become a wasteful flood instead of a fruitful irrigation. Just at that critical moment, in 1895, Lord Acton was sent here as Professor. He gave us such leadership as we then sorely needed, such as is no longer a necessity to the long-established and well-ordered school of to-day.

The splendid development of Cambridge history was not indeed due to Acton alone. The reflected glory of Maitland's work, done under the ægis of the Cambridge Law School, was of great service to the History School as well. And the organization of that school, to cope with ever-increasing numbers without lowering the standards of teaching and research—a difficult and heavy task—was performed by men who are still among us, whom for that reason I do not name. Nevertheless those men are the foremost to assert that the coming of Acton to Cambridge at that particular juncture was a fact of the first consequence.

His advent might be described in the line written by a Cambridge poet about an earlier renaissance of study in this university:

" When Learning like a stranger came from far."

A sage of immense and mysterious distinction, famous in old Continental controversies—of which many in England got their first clear notion as a result of the talk that his coming here aroused—a traveller from the antique lands of European statecraft, religion and learning, with the brow of Plato above the reserved and epigrammatic lips of the diplomatist, we yet found him ready to show personal kindness to every genuine student of history, from Maitland and Cunningham to the humblest freshman. In his college rooms we were all made welcome, singly and by troops, wedged in between the bookshelves containing part of his famous collection that now has a place apart in the University Library. The History School, then one-tenth of its present size, was so small that he was able to come into personal contact with a very large proportion of its members. Each man could receive individual counsel and encouragement in his own work. And collectively we learnt to hold our heads high; under Acton's leadership we did not care how proud we were, for he had excited the imagination of the whole university, and indeed of the country at large. The Cambridge History School was destined in any case to become a big school, but it was largely owing to his arrival at that critical moment that it became a great school.

Acton was succeeded in 1902 by Professor Bury. The heroism with which Bury struggled against ill-health in carrying out his great works of scholarship was a triumph of the zeal for learning over fleshly ills, such as we had noted in the case of Maitland. In knowledge of the history of many races and lands, written in many tongues, Bury was not unworthy to succeed Acton. In productivity as an author the younger man surpassed the older. Acton will live to posterity in a few articles contributed to magazines and in the posthumously published notes of his Cambridge lectures, which display his peculiar power enough to make us long for the unwritten masterpiece of which he dreamed. Bury's published work, on the other hand, is his best title to fame.

Acton bore his immense weight of learning if not lightly at least gallantly. He loved to be dramatic—he could not bear to spoil a good story in the telling—and he was a strong partisan, none the less because his party in Church and State might be said to have consisted of himself alone. His lasting reputation will not depend upon the proved accuracy of all his statements. Bury had fewer temptations of this kind, and his early training in the old-fashioned school of classical linguistic scholarship had equipped him with a mind of unrivalled accuracy in detail. There are diversities of gifts. In Acton there was a width of outlook on the drama of history, a deep insight into the effect of principles upon action and of ideas upon events, a sense of great issues and their significance, a passionate feeling about right and wrong which often flared up from under his dignified and reserved manner of speech. But different as were the powers and temperaments of these two men, they had one marked peculiarity in common, besides matchless erudition — I mean the value they attached to freedom of opinion, and their open partisanship of that cause in every epoch of history. Acton indeed laid most stress upon the evil of coercing conscience, Bury on the evil of fettering the search for truth.[1]

Since my absence from Cambridge corresponds almost exactly with that quarter of a century during which Bury held the professorship, and since many of you have been in residence during most of those years, I will not be so superfluous as to inform you of the manner in which the Cambridge History School grew up, from the vigorous sapling that Acton tended, into the tree with many strong branches under which we sit to-day. It is the duty of a great school like ours to fling its net wide, and to give light and leading on different periods and different aspects of history. In that respect I do not think that much fault can be found with us at present. The series of volumes known as the *Cambridge Histories*, initiated by Lord Acton, though by no means all written by Cambridge men, emanate from here, and they cover a wide ground. It is true that in losing Bury we have lost our high place in Byzantine scholarship, not, I hope, for long. But those who strive to solve the difficult riddles of Anglo-Saxon history still have good reason to look towards Cambridge. And our walls contain mediæval historians of wide fame and influence. Students of European and British affairs, political and diplomatic, from the latter part of the eighteenth century to the present age, have peculiar personal advantages here to-day; they also, I may remind you, enjoy the material advantage of the overflow of Diplomatic and Colonial

---

[1] Two very interesting notes on Bury and his views of history will be found in the *Cambridge Historical Journal*, October 1927, vol. ii., No. 2.

# THE PRESENT POSITION

Documents from the Public Record Office in London into the safe receptacle of the old Cambridge Prison.[1]

To the revival in naval history, begun by Mahan nearly forty years ago, Cambridge men have made great contributions; it does not exhaust the list to name Julian Corbett, whom we have so recently lost. The impulse that Maitland gave to the history of our Laws and Constitution is still vigorously alive in his old university, though its greatest living exponent is at Oxford. The tradition that Cunningham began is strong among us yet; indeed the presence of the brilliant School of Political Economy founded by Alfred Marshall, and the mathematical and scientific atmosphere of Newton's university, help economic history to flourish here at home. In the mechanical age in which we live, with the centre of national interest shifted to economic questions, economic history is becoming increasingly popular and important, and Cambridge is no loser by that.

The connecting link between economic and political history is social history — that is to say, the history of classes and modes of life, with their accompanying habits of thought. It would scarcely be suitable as a separate subject in the tripos, but it would be a misfortune if for that reason it suffered neglect. Works like those of Dill on the society of the Roman Empire, of Graham on eighteenth-century Scotland, and of a living French historian on later phases of English society are among the most fascinating and important additions to recent history. It is to be hoped that economic and political historians will give increasingly serious treatment to the social scene which in each successive period of the world's affairs arises out of economic conditions and governs political events. On that social ground economic and political historians can meet, and they will have much to tell one another. The interest of the present-day

[1] See *Cambridge Historical Journal*, vol. i., No. 1, 1923, pp. 113-117, for Mr Temperley's communication on this subject. Students will find in the old Cambridge Prison duplicates for the diplomatic history of the nineteenth century and unique materials for colonial history, especially from George III. to Victoria.

public is visibly turning to social history—to everyday things in the past.

It was a Cambridge man—Macaulay—who powerfully directed historical attention, in the third chapter of his *History*, towards the social life going on behind the drums and trumpets and Parliamentary debatings, twenty years and more before J. R. Green carried forward the same work so well. Macaulay (as he has put on record in his essay "On History" in his *Miscellaneous Writings*) was in his youth inspired to take interest in the everyday life of our ancestors by the writings of Sir Walter Scott. Scott, who was a great antiquarian before ever he commenced novelist, did more for history, I venture to think, than any professed historian in modern times. Not only did his romances, and all that have since been written in imitation of them by Stevenson and others, popularize our study, and enter homes and hearts where no history-book could find its way: I mean more even than that. Scott had a great contribution of his own to make to the interpretation of history, for it was he who first gave the realism and variety of actual life to the records of the past. It was he who first taught us to think of our ancestors as real human beings with passions and absurdities like our own. It was he also who showed us the difference in mode of life between one epoch and another, and between one class and another in times gone by. Gibbon may or may not have been the greatest of all historical artists; in any case he is the most perfect within his strict limitations. But because he lived before Sir Walter, his stately perfection has in it as little of the variety and warmth of life as the no less perfect Parthenon frieze. Scott gave to history "another heart and other pulses."

The Cambridge History School now occupies a position of national importance. In addition to those few who may become historians by profession, a larger number of young men destined for the ordinary avocations of the world are educated by the history tripos than by any other of the schools which here uphold the tradition and spirit of the humanities in friendly rivalry to the ever-increasing domain of scientific study. To maintain a just balance between the two great aspects of intellectual activity must be an object of anxious care to such a university as ours. And the balance between the humanities and physical science now depends upon history. If it were not for the existence of the History School, the liberal education which letters give would be obtainable by youth only in the strictly linguistic schools. And those schools, important as they are, no longer suffice alone to maintain the cultural traditions of English civilization in an age of rapidly disappearing landmarks.

The eighteenth and nineteenth centuries were a great period for the higher civilization of our island, partly because letters and learning were then closely allied. Before the eighteenth century opened, men of learning had already acquired the habit of writing in English instead of Latin; from that time forward, therefore, their appeal lay not to the learned only, but to the better educated part of the reading public as a whole. The *Dissertation on the Letters of Phalaris*, written in the controversial English of which Bentley at his best was so great a master, was one of the earlier of these appeals. A couple of generations later the movement produced the masterpiece of Gibbon, who wrote for the delight of squires and statesmen a work of historical scholarship that still holds its own in the universities. Meanwhile every gentleman was brought up on a classical education which, whatever its limitations, had the supreme merit of combining in one scheme of study great literature and great history. The common people, it is true, shared only indirectly in the classical culture of the upper class, but they read the Bible instead. Thus the history and literature of the Græco-Roman and of the ancient Hebrew civilizations were the daily food of the English mind. No wonder, then, that we had a golden age of imaginative and literary civilization. It was from this old and richly prepared soil that sprang the great poets, historians and men of letters of the nineteenth century.

These conditions have changed. Though we still have the classics and the Bible, they no longer fill the place they once held. What is the imaginative and intellectual life of England getting in their stead? I do not mean to answer that question in a pessimistic manner merely by asking it. The answer must needs be a long one, which I cannot even attempt to give here, except as regards that part of it which directly concerns ourselves—to wit, the present-day conditions of teaching and writing history. On that subject I should like, in the remaining limits of the hour-glass, to offer a few remarks.

What is the use of history? Whereas the discoveries of physical scientists have importance as means towards material ends—military, medical, industrial and agricultural—on the other hand historical discoveries have scarcely any value except in so far as they educate the mind, stimulate thought, or intensify intellectual emotion. Through the application of physical science, life on the globe is multiplied, prolonged, destroyed. No historical discoveries can have any such effects. But history can make people wiser, and it can give them intellectual pleasure of a very high order indeed. If this is the case, then it appears to me that history is already in danger, and may in each succeeding decade be in greater danger, of wasting much of its force by not knowing well enough what to do with the ever-increasing mass of facts that it accumulates with such admirable zeal and skill. All over Europe and America thousands of devoted workers give their lives to accumulating historical knowledge, which is garnered in books, monographs and learned periodicals. Much of this accumulated knowledge is indeed presented, either at first or second hand, in a most interesting manner and so fulfils its end; but much of it seems to be printed only to remain unused, because a sufficient proportion of time and energy is not given to bringing out the interest latent in the facts discovered and recorded. I know that this is more easily said than done. To some extent the difficulty is inherent in the nature of the case. But there are, I think, various lines on which people are seeking to improve this state of things, and are actually improving it, not least here at Cambridge.

In the first place it is the endeavour here to teach undergraduates not out of text-books of indifferent value, but out of books old and new, each of which has some intellectual or literary merit. The great value of the classical education upon which England throve so well from the time of Colet until almost our own day was the quality of the books which it put into the hands of students. History cannot, perhaps, put before its students books that we can rate as high as the whole library of Greek and Latin literature, but it can, if it so chooses, provide them with many works of high intellectual quality. Swift once wrote a word which educationists should bear in mind: " If a rational man," says the Dean, "reads an excellent author with just application he shall find himself extremely improved, and perhaps insensibly led to imitate that author's perfections, although in a little time he shall not remember one word in the book, nor even the subject it handled: for books give the same turn to our thoughts and way of reasoning that good and ill company does to our behaviour and conversation, without either loading our memories or making us even sensible of the change" (*Letter to a Young Clergyman*).

In all ways it is necessary to make the young student feel that history is at once a stimulation and a satisfaction of intellectual curiosity; that it is a process of thought, not a mere learning by rote. Books have to be chosen and examinations set with that end in view. I believe that the efforts made in this direction of recent years have not been unblessed. A good test of the success or failure of a history school is the proportion of its former students who in afterlife read history for pleasure. Statistics on that point can, I fear, never be available, but I would give a great deal to have them, in the case of the former students of a number of selected universities.

In this connection I would plead that history should not lose touch with its own past. The works of great historians of former times ought to be known not only by name but by use. They should not always be relegated to the dust-heap because on certain points they have been supplemented or corrected by works of smaller intellectual power. Students of English literature are not in the habit of confining their reading to the neo-Georgian poets; and although history is less perennial than poetry, it is in its higher manifestations not so ephemeral as some people are inclined to suppose. We historians also have our heritage, not least in England. The doctrine of the permanent value of great historians was finely enforced by Bury when he re-edited Gibbon, to help keep him in use for modern students.

Since history consists not only in collecting facts about the past, but in thinking about them, old fashions of historical thought are not to be neglected. They often serve as a useful corrective to the fashion of our own age, which is not the quintessence of all that has gone before, but merely the latest mode, with its strong points certainly, but also, we may be sure, with its weak spots as well. Besides some great names that I have already mentioned, there are historians and biographers, such as Sorel, Lecky, Creighton, Symonds, Dicey, Gardiner, Morley, Jessopp, Parkman, Motley, Ranke, Gregorovius, Taine, Tocqueville, Guizot, and many more, who have things to suggest to us, all the more valuable because we may not hear them from contemporaries. The succession of attitudes adopted by the men of the eighteenth and nineteenth centuries towards the past is in itself no unimportant part of history.

Among books written before the eighteenth century, in days when the study of the past laboured under great disadvantages, the historical literature of most educational value for us is, perhaps, the contemporary memoir of passing events, such as Burnet and Clarendon, de Comines and Froissart. Can a man be said to have had a liberal education in English history if he has never read some at least of the nobler passages in Clarendon? And those magnificent political controversies—if we give them no higher title—conducted by Milton and Burke are part of the young history student's birthright as an Englishman; to know something of them he may well be expected to spare a few hours from learning so many more clauses of broken treaties out of text-books.

I will not waste my time and yours by dilating on the importance of research as the basis of any history worthy of the name. That needs no proof and requires no emphasis. It is our business to provide for it here, and I am happy to think that of recent years ampler provision has been made at Cambridge to help the ablest of our young people to travel and engage in original work immediately after their first degree. Authors should sow their wild oats young. Some wild oats, indeed, like Bryce's University Prize Essay, *The Holy Roman Empire*, bring forth a hundredfold of excellent grain.

If the seminar be held as alien to the genius of this university, the friendship of older with younger students is not alien to our traditions. I have already spoken of the encouragement and help Lord Acton gave to so many. And at the present day one of the most important functions of the History School here is the help given in an unofficial way to the man or woman setting out for the first time on original work. The Cambridge University Historical Society exists in large part to foster such personal relations between the more experienced and the younger hands.

But the young historian soon requires help outside his own university. Whether in the British Museum, the Record Office, the Bodleian, or wherever it may be in this country or, as I have abundantly found, in foreign countries, he will experience the seldom-failing kindness, and profit by the skill and knowledge of the keepers of public libraries and records. They are a class of historian to whom we others are bound by warm ties of affection and gratitude.

But most of all, the young historian must depend on his mother-wit and his own initiative, for which no organization of research and no kindness of older persons can ever provide a substitute. Historians are born, not manufactured.

The universities stand in a more important and direct relation to historical production than in former times. The days have gone by when history was written chiefly by men-of-the-world, publicists and beneficed clergymen, for a leisured class with large and learned libraries in their country seats. In those days the universities of England were few and inactive, and even when, in the nineteenth century, they awoke from slumber, it was not until the close of the Victorian era that history became an important part of their work. But to-day society has undergone great changes, and the conditions of intellectual production have changed accordingly. History is now written for the most part by men and women who have been trained in history at the universities, and very largely by persons living upon academic endowment; while the serious reading public is no longer the upper or the middle class as such, but clever persons of all classes. The problem of historical writing to-day is, therefore, to establish a satisfactory contact between the academically trained historians and those who should be their readers, scattered all over the country in various callings and stations of life. It is not altogether an easy task. In old days the writers and readers of history had a common background and common standards—those of a well-educated but not over-learned aristocracy. To-day the writers may sometimes be too academic and the readers not academic enough for purposes of mutual understanding. "The writer is one, and the reader is another," says the Eastern proverb.

# THE PRESENT POSITION

Yet the case is by no means hopeless. For many of the readers have themselves been at universities, or are undergoing academic training by adult education. And not the least important class of reader is the schoolmaster and schoolmistress, who by the nature of their profession have a quasi-academic outlook. If the universities are the fountain-heads of history to-day, the schoolrooms are the rivulets by which the water is disseminated from the fountain-heads over the land. The Historical Association and its organ *History* form one of the most useful links between the universities and the schools.

The relation of history to education is not less important than its relation to literature, and modern educationists are making the same demand as the modern literary world. Both schoolmasters and ordinary readers are asking historians not to be merely learned, but to remember the hungry sheep. What are we to say to this demand, and how far, if at all, is it inconsistent with the academic ideals which it is our duty to maintain at a university? The answer to that question will be given in different terms by each of us, and I have no wish to make any pronouncement upon it with any claim to authority or orthodoxy, but only to express some of my own feelings on the subject. It is, of course, impossible for an historian to give too much, or even enough, time to research, but it seems to me not impossible that he may sometimes give proportionately too much of his time and mental energy to research itself, at the expense of the thought and art that should be devoted to making use of the results of research. We have, as historians, not only to collect facts, but to think about them; and we have also to weave the facts and our thoughts upon them into some form by which others will profit.

There are indeed, and there ought to be, many kinds of historian and many kinds of history. Subdivision of labour is required in history as in other forms of human effort. There are also several kinds of reading public, of which the more select is the more important, but of which none

194

is wholly negligible. Some distinguished historians have deliberately written two books on the same subject, one for the learned and another for a wider class. That is one way of honestly facing a difficult problem. But perhaps the highest ideal of history will always remain the volume that satisfies both the learned and the general reader. There are in fact as many possible solutions to the problem as there are men fit to solve it.

In any case I am sure that historians could not see with indifference the popular presentation of history pass mainly into the hands of others. We welcome the assistance of allies from the realms of literature or journalism, and applaud, while we criticize, their success with historical themes. But their success is a challenge to us, and an encouraging reminder of the growing interest in history among the educated and half-educated democracy of all classes to-day. The immediate future is full of possibility and hope for historians, and they are in many different ways rising to the call and to the challenge of the age.

I will say no more of the theory of the question. Atmosphere has more influence on practice than any theory. Let us put the case then in terms of atmosphere. The problem of presenting the results of historical research to the educational world and to the reading public may best find its solution, and is already beginning to find its solution, in an atmosphere such as we breathe in this ancient university; where literature and learning still go hand in hand; where lucid self-expression with the pen is regarded as a necessary part of a liberal education; where intellectual and literary traditions and careful standards of thought and speech are more respected than in the market-place; where historians are not ignorant of poetry and literature, and where students of language and literature are not ignorant of history; where the schools of natural science, by their neighbourhood and example, help to keep us historians in touch with the modern world and with the active business of research, discovery and production, without affecting our own loyalty to the standard of humane letters.

The appeal of history to us all is in the last analysis poetic. But the poetry of history does not consist of imagination roaming at large, but of imagination pursuing the fact and fastening upon it. That which compels the historian to " scorn delights and live laborious days " is the ardour of his own curiosity to know what really happened long ago in that land of mystery which we call the past. To peer into that magic mirror and see fresh figures there every day is a burning desire that consumes and satisfies him all his life, that carries him each morning, eager as a lover, to the library and the muniment-room. It haunts him like a passion of almost terrible potency, because it is poetic. The dead were and are not. Their place knows them no more and is ours to-day. Yet they were once as real as we, and we shall to-morrow be shadows like them. In men's first astonishment over that unchanging mystery lay the origins of poetry, philosophy and religion. From it too is derived in more modern times this peculiar call of the spirit, the type of intellectual curiosity that we name the historical sense. Unlike most forms of imaginative life it cannot be satisfied save by facts. In the realm of history, the moment we have reason to think that we are being given fiction instead of fact, be the fiction ever so brilliant, our interest collapses like a pricked balloon. To hold our interest you must tell us something we believe to be true about the men who once walked the earth. It is the fact about the past that is poetic; just because it really happened, it gathers round it all the inscrutable mystery of life and death and time. Let the science and research of the historian find the fact, and let his imagination and art make clear its significance.

DATE DUE